Act Normal

MEMOIR OF A STUMBLING BLOCK

Kristy Burmeister

Flipped Mitten Press

Copyright © 2017 by Kristy Burmeister.

All rights reserved. No part of this publication may be reproduced, distributed or transmitted in any form or by any means, including photocopying, recording, or other electronic or mechanical methods, without the prior written permission of the author, except in the case of brief quotations embodied in critical reviews and certain other noncommercial uses permitted by copyright law.

All Scripture quotations, unless otherwise indicated, are taken from the Holy Bible, New International Version®, NIV®. Copyright ©1973, 1978, 1984, 2011 by Biblica, Inc.™ Used by permission of Zondervan. All rights reserved worldwide. www.zondervan.com The "NIV" and "New International Version" are trademarks registered in the United States Patent and Trademark Office by Biblica, Inc.™

"What a Friend We Have in Jesus" lyrics by Joseph M. Scriven, 1855. Public Domain.

Author's Note: I've done my best to present these events fairly and accurately. Where possible, I've validated my memories with pictures, records, research, and interviews. Some dialogue is recreated, based on actual conversations. The name of my hometown in Arkansas has been changed. The names of most people involved have been changed to protect their privacy.

Kristy Burmeister/Flipped Mitten Press

Book Layout ©2017 BookDesignTemplates.com

Cover Design by Laura Hogg

Cover photograph copyright © Sascha Burkard / Shutterstock. All Rights Reserved.

Act Normal/ Kristy Burmeister. —1st ed.

ISBN 978-0-9995700-0-5

Contents

Prologue	1
Part One	7
Part Two	167
Part Three	213
Part Four	273
Epilogue	301

*To my family, who lived it with me.
To all other survivors—of predators and the
communities that shelter them—who have lived it too.*

Prologue

**JUNE 2015
PINE CREEK, ARKANSAS**

*The wind blows to the south
and turns to the north;
round and round it goes,
ever returning on its course.*

—Ecclesiastes 1:6

A/C blasts my face as I flip the passenger-side visor down to check my makeup again. I've spent more time than usual creating this protective barrier between them and me, but the humidity is melting my foundation and curling my hair. I'd forgotten how oppressive Ozark air can be.

Giving up on my face, I punch the radio button with my knuckle. "Danger Zone" blares through the speakers, and I turn to my sister. "Seriously?"

Angela doesn't look away from the road. "Well, guess that works."

Laughter bursts from us at the same time, and I worry the tears forming in my eyes will streak my eyeliner.

Morning sunlight flickers into the car as we drive past limestone bluffs and tree-filled hollers. Angela's dark brown hair is still wet from her morning shower, and it shines when the sun hits it. She's dressed sensibly, as always. Jeans and a modest top.

I'd packed a conservative floral blouse and long skirt for today, but ten minutes before we left the hotel, I pulled on a pair of skinny jeans and a blue snakeskin print top instead.

With my frizzy blonde hair, I look a little wild. I figure these people already think I'm a little wild, so why not just roll with it?

Our tiny, silver car dips and turns along the mountain road until we hit Pine Creek, Arkansas. It's a town we barely recognize, so we rely on Angela's muscle memory to make the right turns. Here and there, a building sparks a memory, but we question them all. "Wait. Maybe that's *not* where we used to rent videos. But it's got to be somewhere around here."

We drive past the abandoned Pizza Hut where Angela had her first job. I used to call in a pizza order on my way home at least once a week. If Angela was working, my pizza was safe. Otherwise, Daniel might slip it into the takeout box upside down on me.

Angela wants to stop by our old high school, so we make a quick stop there. It's the same short, one-story building we grew up in, right across the street from the Sonic where I'd worked as a carhop my senior year, skating Route 44s out to people's cars.

In front of the school building, each graduating class has a slab with their names engraved into it. We find my name with the class of 1999, but Angela isn't listed with the class of 2000.

She reaches into the car, rips a piece of paper out of my notebook, and writes, "*Angela WAS HERE 1996–2000 regardless of your plaque!*" She places it on the senior sidewalk, where her name would have gone, and takes a picture with her phone.

She knows she shouldn't be listed. Still, I get it. That feeling of being erased and forgotten, like you never mattered.

I'm feeling guilty enough to make promises. "When I have some money, I'll buy you a plaque and make them put it out. And yours will be way cooler than these other ones."

She glances at me out of the corner of her eye. "It better be."

Our rental car pulls away from the school and heads back through town. We take a hard left onto Old Highway 83, and I feel a little like throwing up. Or passing out. Or yanking the car door open and rolling to safety.

We have a plan. After discarding my original idea of bursting through the double doors of our old church shouting, "We're back, bitches!" we settled on showing up during Sunday school. If anyone asks, we'll tell them we're flying out of Little Rock that afternoon, which is both true and a good excuse if we decide to leave in a hurry. All our talk about strategy makes it feel like we're infiltrating enemy headquarters.

The church sign pops up over a hill on our right: Pine Creek Mennonite Brethren Church. "Take a deep breath," she tells me.

I've already taken three.

Part One

**AUGUST 1999
PINE CREEK, ARKANSAS**

*If an enemy were insulting me,
I could endure it;
if a foe were rising against me,
I could hide.
But it is you, a man like myself,
my companion, my close friend,
with whom I once enjoyed sweet fellowship
at the house of God,
as we walked about
among the worshipers.*

—Psalm 55:12-14

CHAPTER ONE

My bedroom was a disappointing crime scene. No overturned furniture. No slashed mattress. No dramatic evidence an unwanted visitor had been there. It would have been easier to swallow if he'd bothered to make his presence more obvious by smashing my CD player. Or he could have really done me a favor and spray-painted his name in bright-orange letters across my walls. But he didn't tag my walls or leave a signed note or muddy print from a one-of-a-kind boot in the middle of my carpet.

The day before, I'd helped drywall a house with Mennonite Disaster Service in Oklahoma City. That night, Angela found me on the front steps of our Oklahoma host church, picking drywall mud off my new engagement ring. She said Dad was on the phone because someone had broken into our house. I was sure she'd heard wrong until Dad confirmed her story with one clarification. Only *my* room had been broken into. Being singled out made me feel like I was walking around naked, but that was probably the whole point.

Our church youth group had cut the service trip short this morning and piled into a van to head home to Arkansas. My legs ached from being crunched up in the back seat for six hours. I felt a little light-headed, moving from the van to the mosquito-infested parking lot, through the air-conditioned living room, and into my muggy bedroom within the past few minutes. At least my boyfriend, Ben, was right behind me. He'd catch me if I passed out.

This wasn't the kind of thing that happened in real life, and it especially didn't happen out in the country. We were supposed to be safe in Pine Creek. Dad never even bothered to lock our front door most nights because who'd ever break into the pastor's house?

I tried to ignore that neck-tickling sensation of being overly exposed and got to work. The police wanted me to check my room to see if anything had been stolen, so I scanned the room while Ben stood in the doorway, still in his work coveralls, as I carried out my Very Official Inspection.

Rumpled sheets. Lace-curtain panel shoved to the side, caught between the mattress and wall. White mini blinds hung cockeyed, halfway up the dark window. Before leaving for Oklahoma, I'd left a pile of folded laundry on my bed, but now it was scattered around the floor.

My room was different than I'd left it, but not different enough for the police to notice. I *could* have knocked the laundry over myself. I *could* have yanked the blinds up. The knot solidifying in my stomach demanded a better ransacking than this.

"Anything gone?" Ben asked, removing his ball cap and running a hand just under his sweat-soaked, dirty-blond widow's peak.

How could I tell? I didn't keep an inventory list tacked up on my wall. And I didn't have the most organized room, especially since I was in the middle of packing to move into the dorms. It didn't *look* like anything was missing. Half-packed cardboard boxes still sat in a corner. My scholarship letter from the University of Central Arkansas was taped proudly above my desk, along with a few prom pictures. All my old dolls were still covered in dust and displayed on a shelf above my mirror.

The humidity was getting to me. The air was too thick, and I couldn't suck in enough oxygen. I pulled the end of my tie-dyed T-shirt up to wipe my oily face.

Ben watched with a sad little look, but didn't say anything. I closed the short gap between us and hid my face in his neck.

It's never fair when someone breaks into another person's house, but this struck me as particularly unfair. I'd given up part of my summer to go to Oklahoma to work with Mennonite Disaster Service. While I was in another state, rebuilding tornado-damaged houses with Ben, Dad, and Angela, a man climbed through my bedroom window, even though I'd always been nice to him.

Ben wrapped both solid arms around me. When he moved, the smell of sweat and Stetson cologne mixed with the vanilla candles on my desk. From down the hall, Dad's deep voice took turns with Mom's.

After one last deep breath, I pushed off Ben's chest and led him into the living room where my parents,

Angela, and her boyfriend, Daniel, were going over what happened.

Dad leaned his long frame against the front door in mud-covered, knee-hole-ripped jeans. Black hair poked out beneath the dirty, blue ball cap he wore on every MDS service trip. Two heads below him, Mom stood just off to his side with her arms crossed in front of a baggy, blue T-shirt that said "Jesus Christ" in gold block letters.

Ben took a seat on our rust-colored couch with Angela and Daniel, and I jerked my thumb at my taller-than-me younger sister so she'd scoot over and let me sit next to him. The four of us squeezed in so tight, the Skoal can in Ben's pocket dug into my hip.

Normally, Mom parked herself in the recliner, but she was too fidgety for that now. She'd met us on the front porch when we pulled up to the house. I asked if she was OK, and she replied with, "The police said to check your room and let them know if anything's missing," which didn't answer my question at all.

Mom hadn't gone to Oklahoma with the rest of us. She was the only person home when the break-in happened. I asked her to start from the beginning because I'd only heard parts of the story, thirdhand (passed from Dad to Angela to me), and it didn't make sense. How could a situation I'd brushed off as slightly inconvenient turn into this?

CHAPTER TWO

Mom's feet shuffled around under her. She was so agitated, I had a hard time imagining her being any more upset the other night, when the break-in actually happened. "I had a migraine. I *know* I locked the front door before I went to bed. And I checked it again when I got back up to take some ibuprofen."

"But he didn't come in through the front door, right?" I asked.

She shook her head without looking at me. "The police found the screen popped off your window."

He'd climbed in through my bedroom window, which meant he'd stepped on my bed to get through. I'd have to change my sheets.

Angela wanted to know when she'd called the police.

"When I heard him."

"I thought you were asleep," I said.

Mom leaned forward, resting her folded arms against the back of the recliner. "I kept waking up."

She always had a hard time sleeping when Dad wasn't home. At some point that night, she woke up and walked across the hall into the bathroom. She was only half awake, in the way a light-sensitive person with a throbbing migraine would be.

"Your door was closed one of the times I got up," she said, looking at me. "I opened it and went back to bed, but the next time I got up, it was closed again."

"So, you called the police?" Angela asked.

Dad took out his pocketknife and started scraping drywall mud out from under his fingernails. He'd already heard most of this over the phone.

Mom gave a little laugh and rolled her eyes. "Right. Call the police and tell them my doors are closing themselves. Yeah. That wouldn't sound crazy at all. And maybe I just *thought* I'd opened it. My head hurt so bad I wasn't sure, so I just went back to bed."

"You went back to bed? When my door closed itself?" I looked over at Ben for some backup on how scary closing doors could be, but he just gave me a little grimace. It wasn't his place to contradict my mother.

"I didn't know for sure anyone had closed it."

"Still . . ."

Dad looked up from his fingernails long enough to meet my eye and give a low, "Kristy."

Ben moved his hand to my knee and dragged a rough thumb back and forth across my skin, trying to settle me down before I popped off and got myself into trouble.

I turned to Angela and Daniel. Daniel never would have intruded into the conversation, but his dark head gave me a "good question" sort of twitch. Angela shot me the same look I gave her when I was trying to watch TV and she wouldn't stop drumming on the end table.

I let it go. A fully awake person without a jackhammer attacking their brain might have been a little spooked, but I knew it was hard to think straight in the middle of a migraine. "So, why'd you call the police?"

She'd heard a thunk coming from my bedroom. "That's when I knew someone was in the house."

But migraines make people sensitive to noise, and it could have been squirrels on the roof or a skunk out in the yard or any kind of thing you hear when you live down a dirt road.

"So, you called the police."

"Well, I called Travis first, but he didn't answer." Travis was our new youth group leader, and also worked for the police department in town. She figured he'd come over and check the house for her, and then she wouldn't have to deal with any embarrassment if it really had just been a squirrel on the roof.

After a few unsuccessful phone calls to Travis and a few more thunks from the other side of the bedroom wall, she called the sheriff's department.

"Did they find anything?" I asked.

Her eyes narrowed. "They wouldn't even dust for fingerprints. Said it was too humid, which is bullcrap."

Ben tensed a little beside me, and Dad looked up again to stare disapprovingly at Mom's use of "crap." We didn't use cusswords like that in our house.

I'd never heard of the fingerprint humidity rule either. "They didn't do *anything*?"

"They walked through the house with me. Thought I was just some hysterical woman. I heard a noise and got scared because my husband wasn't home. The only thing they found was your window screen."

And the laundry all over my floor. And the messy bed. And the half-open blinds. But none of that would have looked like evidence to anyone other than me.

"That idiot dispatcher couldn't hear me. I had to yell over the phone to give her our address. I know he heard me and went back out the window. If she hadn't been so dang deaf, they would've caught him."

Maybe he *had* heard her through the bedroom wall. The parsonage walls were thin, proven by the scuff marks on my side of the wall from when I'd get irritated with my parents for watching TV late at night and throw whatever was handy at the wall to get them to turn it down a notch.

If it'd been me, I was sure I wouldn't have let him hear me call the police. I would've stretched the phone cord into the closet and shut the door before making any phone calls. That's what they did in movies so the killer wouldn't hear them. I looked down and imagined being the not-so-helpless victim who knows she can't fight off an intruder, so she outsmarts him instead.

"*What* did they do?" Dad boomed, drawing me out of my daydream.

Ben eased his hand off my knee and sat up straighter, hands on his own legs. I looked over at Angela for a clue about what I'd missed, but all I got from her was a wide-eyed stare.

Mom repeated herself. "They *yelled* at me."

"The police?" I asked.

"Elmer and Jackie," she said, looking at Ben. This was

not good. This was really, really not good.

"Are you sure they yelled at you?" I gave Ben a quick side-eyed glance. No wonder he'd tensed up. Mom was talking about his father and older sister. "I mean, why would they yell at *you*?"

Since all of us met at the church and rode in a van together on the trip to Oklahoma, Ben had left his car parked in the gravel lot between my house and the church. After the police left, Mom was too scared to stay in the house, so she borrowed Ben's car and drove it over to Travis and Pam's so she could stay the night with them.

The next morning, she called Elmer. "I didn't want him to drive by the church, see the car gone, and think someone stole it."

Elmer had served as assistant pastor of Pine Creek Mennonite Brethren Church for years before Dad was hired as the pastor. He'd known my family for four years, and I'd been in a relationship with his son for two of those years. When I was sixteen, and selling handmade greeting cards to raise money for a short-term mission trip, Elmer had walked up to me after church and handed me a bulletin. Inside was $200 and a note right above the order of service that said, "For your trip." I couldn't imagine him being anything other than supportive of a scared woman, all on her own, dealing with a home invasion—especially when that woman was his pastor's wife and future daughter-in-law's mother.

Mom had the same idea. When she told him about the break-in, she thought he'd say, "Don't worry about it," or ask if she was OK or insist she stay the night at his house until we all got back from Oklahoma.

"He was mad I took the car without asking first," she said.

Ben's much older sister, Jackie, was with Elmer when Mom called and heard his side of the conversation. Jackie demanded details, which Elmer relayed to Mom. What happened? What did she hear? Was she sure someone was there? Did she see who it was?

Mom still had a migraine, and she hadn't slept since that thunk woke her up, and Jackie was her friend, and Elmer was mad about the car, and she didn't want him to be mad, and she had no reason to think they wouldn't believe her, so she told them, "He smelled like Ray."

We all knew what she meant by that. Ray lived out in the woods, in a shack without running water. If you caught wind of that unique stench, Ray was either about to walk into the room or had just walked out. (Or, in this case, climbed out.)

Mom said Jackie let loose with a high-pitched shriek of, "It was *not* Ray!" before Mom could say anything else about it. Ray was Jackie's friend, and she would *never* be friends with the type of man who'd break into the pastor's house.

Mom tried to defend herself by telling them Ray had been following me around all summer, even though Dad had told him to stay away from me. And Ray had shown up at the youth group's car wash a couple of weeks ago, just to ask who was and wasn't going on our MDS trip to Oklahoma. And Ray had spent the night at our house before, so he knew where my room was, and Mom was plenty familiar with his distinct smell. But they didn't want to hear it.

At that point, the whole vibe in the room shifted. I stared at Ben, expecting him to say something about his family, but he only said, "I don't mind if you drove the car."

Mom opened her mouth to reply, but Dad exploded instead. He'd been calm about everything until then. Dad didn't tend to get worked up over petty, little things like breaking and entering. Bad guys were going to do bad things, and sometimes good people got in their way, but an assistant pastor shouldn't go and jump all over the pastor's wife for driving away from a crime scene.

Dad strode around the room, too-long arms flailing. He was all "backward hillbillies" and "ignorant hicks" while Angela and I sat next to our two Ozark-born boyfriends while they tried to disappear into the couch.

"Daniel and Ben are *right here*," Angela cut in.

Dad stopped long enough to turn to us. "Well, they need to not be right here. Our family needs to deal with this alone." And to the boys, "Y'all need to go."

Angela and I glared at him for kicking our boyfriends out, but we weren't stupid enough to verbally challenge him. I tried to tug Ben back down when he rose, but he didn't even glance down at me as he obediently stood and rushed out the front door with Daniel.

I didn't understand why two of my favorite people had to leave. The boys *were* family. Ben spent as much time at my house as his, and Daniel even came along on family trips when we'd go to see my grandparents in Texas or Dad's friends in Indiana.

And what was there to deal with? Ray broke into our house. Sure, it was scary and stressful, but he wasn't breaking in right that second. A little spark at the back of my mind wondered if maybe he hadn't broken in, after all. Maybe Mom really had just heard an animal outside and called the police in a panic. The screen on my window wasn't all that sturdy. I kept it that way on purpose. Sometimes I forgot my house key and had to climb through my bedroom window, which was just the right height for me to haul myself up and over the sill.

As Dad continued to come up with new varieties of Ozark-inspired insults, I noticed some magazines partially shoved under the end table beside the couch. They were the wedding magazines Mom had bought for us to flip through. I'd left them on my desk, but maybe she'd gone through them, hunting for reception ideas while I was away. I lifted the stack onto my lap. They were crumpled. Entire pages had been ripped out and shoved back into the cover. I thought about people who got so angry they could rip a phone book in half. What I was holding looked angry.

A skunk didn't sneak in and tear up my magazines. A person had done that. *Ray.* He really climbed through my window. Picked through my laundry. Touched my things.

The knot in my stomach shifted to my chest, and it hurt to breathe, just like when I used to walk to school in Indiana and the icy winter air froze my throat on the

Act Normal

way down.

Why were the magazines hidden under an end table in the living room when Ray was in my bedroom the whole time? I couldn't ask Mom about it while Dad was still on an anti-redneck rampage.

Angela got tired of listening to Dad rant and walked out the front door with her high ponytail swinging behind her. Daniel was still outside. Dad had told him to get out of the house, not off the property. I wanted to leave too, but how could I when it was my bedroom?

Eventually, Dad settled down. By the time he ran out of steam, I'd already figured out how the magazines got from my room to the living room. Nobody had been in the house all day. Mom was at Travis and Pam's, and the rest of us were in a van, driving back from Oklahoma. Ray had a whole day in the house, if he'd wanted it. He'd had enough time to touch everything I owned.

Dad stormed off to make a phone call, and I escaped to straighten up my room. While yanking my fitted sheet off the bed, a thought popped into my head. Ray *must* have heard Mom on the phone with the police. That's why he was gone by the time they showed up. My sheets were all messed up because he had to jump over my bed and scramble out the window.

Maybe, in his hurry to escape, he'd left something behind. It played out in my head. The bumbling crook dives for the open window and snags his foot on the way out. His shoe is stuck! *Oh, forget the shoe*, he thinks, and yanks his foot free, leaving a telltale shoe behind.

I dropped to the floor I hadn't vacuumed in weeks—

maybe months—and peeked under the bed, eager to find evidence. But I didn't find a shoe. There was nothing except the usual under-bed junk.

It was a stupid idea. If he came back to move the magazines, why wouldn't he have grabbed any lost shoes? This was real life, not some detective show. I wasn't going to find any smoking shoes the police missed.

CHAPTER THREE

Every time I rolled over in bed that night, I peeled my sticky arms apart at the elbow. On any other August night, the hall attic fan sucked a breeze in through my open window, but now my window was locked tight. I *hoped* it was locked tight.

I started to recite my silent nightly prayer. *Please protect me and my family.*

When I'd crawled into a bunk bed at our host church in Oklahoma, I'd been so tired from a full day of mudding drywall in the heat, I'd fallen asleep as soon as my head hit the pillow. Without saying my prayer.

That prayer was like a magic spell. I'd started saying a version of it about the time we first moved to Arkansas when I was in the ninth grade, and I'd recited the same prayer, every night, for over four years.

The thing about having such young parents (or maybe the thing about having young parents like mine) is you grow up with a lot of magic around. They met at a discount store in Texas and got married a few months later when Mom was eighteen and Dad was twenty-one. That meant they had the energy to stay up all night and jingle car keys outside our bedroom window so we'd know Santa was out there. Or they'd sneak out and bury the base of an artificial Christmas tree in the ground so we'd think Dad was strong enough to rip a tree up by its roots. Mom bought fake rubber snakes to prank Dad, and Dad juggled fruit in the grocery store, not to entertain us kids, but because *he* was bored with shopping.

I was ten and Angela was nine when we left Texas and our extended family. Mom got *The World Book Encyclopedia: Volume I* out and flipped to Indiana. "See?" she said, pointing to a picture that didn't look anything like a mesquite tree, "Indiana has *real* trees."

Ever since the second grade, when I'd seen a black-and-white picture of a car driving through a redwood tree, my one big dream was to see a forest. I couldn't satisfy myself with scrubby, old mesquite trees when ancient giants existed. I wanted a real forest, like they had up north in Indiana. Living in Indiana would be like living in a real-life fairy tale—all breadcrumbs and gingerbread houses. Angela and I could explore those wild, northern forests. Maybe we'd find some kids who got separated from their family and lost their way. I'd guide them out with my compass and get my picture in the newspaper.

I knew I could do it because I always stayed calm in a crisis. When I was nine, and the field by our house caught fire, I was the only kid who didn't panic. I filled bowls of water for Mom and Aunt Shyrl, grabbed the first-aid directions in case I had to treat any burns, and smacked Angela upside the head with a couch cushion when she started getting hysterical. Calm, cool, and collected. That was me.

Heroic acts like those made me think I might secretly be a fairy tale princess. But I wasn't a princess who sat around waiting to get saved. I always made Angela be *that* princess. I was the princess who climbed our play fort's ladder with my plastic She-Ra helmet on and an invisible sword strapped to my back. I was the kind of princess who saved the other princesses. My parents knew who I really was (probably because a fairy or some ancient book told them, you know, the usual thing), but they didn't want to tell me until I was older. What an awful burden to place on a kid. Knowing you had to save the whole world. But moving to a place with a forest seemed like a reasonable first step toward heroism. All heroes start out in a forest.

But we moved into a tiny apartment in Elkhart, in the middle of a field. A few smallish trees grew down by a creek, but the only time I ventured down there, a boy threw live snakes at me and my friend until we screamed and ran back to her apartment. Indiana turned out to be mostly farmland, and who ever heard of a person enjoying a happily ever after in a cornfield?

When I strode into fifth grade wearing red ropers, some of the kids laughed at me and told me, "Say 'y'all' again," and I would, and they'd laugh at that too. One boy called me Texas instead of Kristy, and I couldn't figure out how that could be an insult since Texas had been its own country and had the best flag out of any state.

My parents found a new kind of magic when they discovered Mennonites. On our first Sunday in a Mennonite church, the pastor talked about love. When we got into the car to go home, my parents turned to each other and both said, "He was talking to *me*!"

The more my parents learned about Mennonites, the more they fell in love with them. That was especially true of Dad. He was fascinated by the Mennonite commitment to pacifism. It was a sign they weren't like so many of the hypocritical Christians out there, who only pretended to follow the Bible.

We'd always been more-or-less Christians (definitely less, though, since we rarely wandered into a church, and my parents had never even baptized us), but when my parents joined the Mennonite Church, we became really-for-real Christians.

At church, they stuck me in the junior youth group. I was the only kid in my Sunday school class who didn't have her own Bible, so the teacher gave me an NIV with a bright-red cover.

Phrases like "swaddling clothes" and "tabernacle" went right over my head. I thought the Ark of the Covenant was Noah's Ark and couldn't figure out how all the animals didn't die because obviously they had to touch it if they were sailing around inside it.

These church people said God had a plan. He was in control of everything. Nothing happened unless God wanted it to happen. God brought my family to Indiana to meet the Mennonites. Otherwise, my parents never would have reaffirmed their faith, and Angela and I would've been destined to grow up as hell-bound heathen humanists.

When I turned twelve, I started getting migraines

almost every day, and if that was part of God's plan, it didn't seem like such a great plan to me. Mom or Dad would have to pick me up early from school most days. I'd half-climb, half-crawl up the stairs to the bedroom I shared with Angela and lie there, listening to the blood behind my eye throb in time to my heartbeat.

Mom and Dad took me to doctors, but they couldn't stop the migraines or the vomiting that came with them. My weight kept going down, and kids at school noticed something was even more off about me than usual. A girl on my bus sat behind me and hit me in the head with whatever was handy. Or she'd come up to me at lunch when we were all lined up to play four square and shove me into the bleachers.

Another girl called me over during PE one day while we were playing soccer out on the muddy field. She was popular, and I wasn't sure what she'd want to say to someone like me, but I ran up to her and three of her friends. "Yeah?"

"Just this." She smeared a glop of mud down my arm, and then turned to one of her friends and said, "Like I was going to wipe it on my pants."

The girls laughed and started walking away. Dad always said to turn it into a joke. It takes a bully's power away if you act like they didn't hurt you.

"Thank you!" I shouted after them, and they turned back to stare at me. "Mud's really good for your skin!"

"She's so weird."

I started vomiting right after breakfast, even when my head hadn't started hurting yet. More doctors. More migraines. More bullies.

It's hard to believe in magic or universal plans when you're in so much pain you want to drive your head through your bedroom wall. And it's hard to believe you're a hero when you can't even defend yourself from junior high bullies.

After we moved to Oklahoma, I got better. That was probably because my stress levels dropped when I left those Yankee bullies back in Indiana, but we'd also started attending a Mennonite Brethren church in Tulsa around the same time, so that's what I pinned it on.

Even though, at fourteen, I was the youngest kid in the high school youth group, all the kids there were nice to me. If I was hanging back, and not participating much, one of the older kids would talk to me or goof off a little and make me laugh so I'd feel more comfortable. I wanted to be like those kids. Confident and kind and funny. Some of the girls carried around a teen devotional Bible, so I saved up my birthday money and bought the same one, along with a burgundy Bible cover. I woke up at 5:00 every morning to do my devotionals and have prayer time before I had to get ready for school. And I was no early bird, so that was some serious devotion right there.

I made friends when I started school in Broken Arrow. Other girls invited me to their houses or to the roller-skating rink on Friday nights. They called me on the phone to talk about boys they liked.

The only black spot was Mom's illness. Right before we moved to Broken Arrow, she caught the stomach flu, but it never went away. She hurt all over, and she threw up all the time. Dad took her to doctors while we were at school, and they tested her for all sorts of things. Sometimes a test would come back with something, but it never explained all her problems. They found a bad gene that could be causing her back pain, but wouldn't cause her to throw up. In the end, they called it fibromyalgia, even though they knew it had to be something else.

Just as I was losing my snake-pranking mother to a mystery illness, the pastor at our church heard about a Mennonite Brethren congregation in a small Arkansas town that needed a pastor. I wasn't excited about leaving my friends, but I was so immersed in all that Bible stuff by that time, I didn't want to irritate God by telling Dad *not* to follow a pastoral call.

When we walked into the little white chapel in Arkansas, white-haired women hugged me and said, "Just call me Grandma." On my first day of school in Pine Creek, three kids came up to me in the cafeteria to say, "You doin' OK? Come find me if you need something," because they thought I looked upset and they actually cared about that. A woman from church drove Angela and me to and from school every day, along with her son, so we wouldn't have to ride the bus. She'd stop at Sonic on half-price drink day and buy us Route 44s, and on my sixteenth birthday, she gave me a gold bracelet and wooden sunflowers she painted because she knew it was my favorite flower.

By sixteen, I was old enough to know magic wasn't real. But God was. This was that plan thing people talked about. If I'd never lived in Indiana and gone through that whole ordeal, my parents never would have run into the Mennonites. Dad never would have gone to seminary and never would have moved us to Oklahoma to plant a church. We'd never have found a Mennonite Brethren church in Tulsa with a pastor who knew about a little church in Arkansas. Our journey from Texas to Indiana to Oklahoma to Arkansas was so convoluted, it *had* to be a miracle.

God knew it was going to be hard on Angela and me with Mom being sick, so he brought us to Pine Creek. To a place where people would love us and take care of us, like we were family. Maybe I was living in a fairy tale after all, and Pine Creek was my happily ever after.

And I'd gone and screwed it up. I'd skipped my prayer—the prayer that kept us safe. Our God was a fickle God, and he'd turn on a dime if I didn't keep up with my nightly litany. Oh, sure, he'd move mountains for our faith, but only if we asked. And maybe, if we failed to ask, he'd take away our blessings to punish us for being ungrateful.

The one night I didn't pray was the night Ray climbed through my window. God allowed his only son to be tortured and killed for my sins, and I couldn't even stay awake for a few minutes to say a prayer. A better Christian wouldn't have fallen asleep before praying, but I hadn't been a very good Christian lately.

During my junior year, I led two Bible studies and saw my friends at the pole. I listened to DC Talk and Newsboys while writing skits to perform in church or at our Saturday youth revival meetings. I was on fire and fired up and freaked out for Jesus and out to save our Bible Belt town.

And who cared if my grades slipped a little because I devoted so much time after school to planning Bible study lessons and writing skits? I might have pulled a D in geometry one semester, but I sure got an A+ in salvation.

Then I started dating Ben, and all that church stuff faded into the background. Making out with him was so much better than writing melodramatic skits about evangelizing everyone in school.

According to some people in our church, even kissing might be a step too far into the devil's grasp, but I knew kissing wasn't wrong. So maybe those adults were just old-fashioned and overreacted to any kind of physical affection. Maybe it wasn't a big deal if we fooled around some. That's what Ben thought. From there, it wasn't a stretch to think, if *that's* OK, then full-on sex was OK too. Which was exactly where my moral compass landed.

Even though I felt plenty justified—we were in love, we were going to get married—I'd still betrayed God. A couple of months before Ben and I started dating, we stood up in front of our church and made a promise. Virginity now. Virginity forever. At least, until we got married and flipped some matrimonial switch, which would make all these now-evil feelings we had healthy and good. Regardless of how right or wrong I was about sex, we'd still broken a promise to God and to our church.

God brought me to Pine Creek, to my first real home, to the boy I was going to marry, and I'd gone and stabbed the Lord in the back. And I'd stabbed him in the back so hard, I hadn't even spoken to him one night. Maybe this was what I deserved for ignoring God.

But there was always forgiveness, right? Anything could be fixed if you tried hard enough. And my parents had a plan that would fix everything.

CHAPTER FOUR

Our church was a postcard-worthy country chapel. Built in 1947 by the Mennonite Brethren, it stood a few miles outside Pine Creek. The sanctuary could squeeze in about one hundred if we added folding chairs down the main aisle, but only about eighty comfortably and only in winter, when we didn't mind the extra body heat.

The church and parsonage were separated by a gravel parking lot, with a beatdown sidewalk running between the two. An overgrown field stretched out behind the parsonage. When we first moved in, Jackie's horses roamed the field, and she told us we could saddle them up and ride anytime we wanted.

The sign on the main road said we were a Mennonite Brethren church, but there was never much of a Mennonite vibe in the place. Since the church had started out as a church plant, nobody in the congregation was ethnically Mennonite.

Ethnic Mennonites have a long history. Their ancestors were Anabaptist martyrs in Europe, persecuted and killed because they wouldn't raise a sword or baptize their infants. Some were tortured. Some were drowned. Some were burned alive. Men could break their bodies, but they couldn't break their faith. Real Christians take persecution and suffering and turn it into four-part harmony. All good Mennonite kids know that.

Our church's lack of Menno cred popped up here and there. Unlike my family, who'd received our Mennonite training in the middle of Indiana's Amish country, most of our church members weren't pacifists. Since many of our members had close family ties to Pentecostal and Assembly of God churches in our area, the congregation was more open to things like faith healing and speaking in tongues than a typical Mennonite church would be.

Mennonite Brethren churches didn't allow women to preach, but compared to some other churches, we were downright progressive. Our women didn't have to cover their heads like conservative Mennonites, and we were even allowed to wear pants, unlike some independent fundamentalist Baptists I knew. We were the lucky ones.

That Sunday morning, church folk stood in clumps around the sanctuary, talking and waiting for the worship service to start. Some men wore dress slacks and crisp shirts while others wore plaid button-up shirts tucked into low-slung, belted jeans that threatened to slide out from under their giant bellies. Women wore sensible knee-length skirts or long, denim skirts that were a good ten years out of fashion. The clothes were evidence of what I loved most about our church. Everyone was welcome. Accountant, factory worker, police officer, optometrist, small-business owner, housekeeper, stay-at-home mother *or* father, all worshipped together under one steeple.

A few of the older women gave me squishy hugs as they walked past. Mom and Dad encouraged us to find family wherever we lived. Family wasn't blood, they said, it was who showed up when you needed them.

Jackie let out a loud laugh as she stood next to Rhonda, their denim skirts melding together. Our new youth group leader, Travis, walked through the side door with his wife and kids. His dark slicked back hair and mustache made him stick out as a police officer, even out of uniform. I felt a little less anxious with him in the room.

Paul, the older, soft-spoken church elder who used to give me rides to play rehearsal after school, stood at the back of the church next to Mike, the stay-at-home father elder who'd helped baptize me in a spring-fed creek two years earlier. I was sure they'd heard about the break-in by now. They glanced over as I walked by, and I gave them a little smile, like I always did.

Act normal.

When Dad finally calmed down after running Ben and Daniel out, he called a state trooper he knew to get advice. The state trooper offered to visit church that morning in uniform. He thought it might make Ray nervous. Maybe it'd trip him up and he'd say something that proved he'd been in my room the other night.

Mom would make the rounds after service and talk to any woman who might listen about the wedding dress we'd picked out. Maybe hearing about my wedding would irk Ray enough to cause an outburst like he'd had two years ago when the exorcists hauled him off. And then everyone would see how unstable he was, and Jackie would shut her trap, and Elmer would apologize, and Ray would go back into the hospital, and it'd all be done with.

Dad told me I only had one job. Act normal. Don't tip Ray off. Act like I don't know about the break-in. Stay out of the whole mess and let the adults handle it.

I hovered around the foyer for as long as possible. The less I had to interact with people, the better. I wasn't sure how normal I could be. How do you act normal around a person who broke into your bedroom?

An hour earlier, I'd been in slightly better shape. I sat on our living room floor with my legs and ankle-length skirt tucked modestly beneath me while the rest of the youth Sunday school class sat in a circle beside me listening to Travis speak. I was too preoccupied to pay any attention to the lesson, though. I kept trying to figure out why Jackie and Elmer had freaked out.

I held a pink Bible on my lap and flipped through its pages like a flipbook. It was new. Elmer had given it to me, on behalf of the church, when I graduated high school three months earlier. My name was embossed on the front, and on the first page, written in blue ink: Presented to Kristy from Pine Creek MB Church. Elmer had called me up front that Sunday, said a few words about adulthood, and placed his hand on my shoulder to lead the congregation as they prayed a blessing over me. Obviously, it didn't stick.

Partway through a flip, I stopped and let the Bible fall open so I could read the page I'd landed on. One section of verses caught my eye. It was part of the Sermon on the Mount, my favorite part of the Bible. I grabbed a yellow highlighter out of the coffee table drawer and marked the passage. I flipped again and landed in 1 Corinthians. Again, I dragged the highlighter across the page and stared at the verses. Given the circumstances, it felt downright prophetic.

When I checked the foyer bulletin board, I knew why. My name was printed under Special Presentation. I'd forgotten all about it. I was supposed to get up in front of the church and present something during the service. When the time came, should I apologize and say I didn't have anything to share? Would that seem fishy? I always did something if my name was down. People would expect it. If I had to act normal, I had to stand up and present *something*.

As I tried to figure out what to do, I walked down the middle aisle toward my pew. Ray's long, dark, shaggy hair sat a few pews behind my friends. I told myself not to turn in his direction as I passed, but some ornery part of my brain snapped my eyes over as I got level with him. His too-wide eyes met mine, and through his overgrown beard, he smirked.

Squeezing in between Ben and Angela, I sat rigid in my pew. Dad stood behind the pulpit and went over the week's announcements. The next potluck was on the 29th, and Dad was sure looking forward to Fern's pies, but what was everyone else going to eat? Polite chuckles mixed with genuine cackles.

Angela, Daniel, and I would usually start passing notes during the announcements while Ben pretended not to notice, but I wasn't in the mood for jokes.

Alma instructed us to open the green hymnal to #260. I stood with my friends and sang with the congregation.

What a friend we have in Jesus,
all our sins and grief to bear.

Voices rose around me. Angela sang quietly to my left and Ben, more loudly, to my right. Booming deep notes bellowed out of the men and ricocheted around my chest. A few scattered women harmonized, and the musically inclined mixed in with those of us who belted out off-key lyrics. Jackie, as always, out-sang everyone.

Have we trials and temptations?
Is there trouble anywhere?
We should never be discouraged;
take it to the Lord in prayer.

Ray's eyes burned into the back of my head. Was the state trooper watching him watch me right now? Or was he bent over his hymnal, singing along and as oblivious to Ray as the rest of the congregation? How many of them knew what had happened? Elmer and Jackie knew. The rest of the church council knew if they did. It wasn't like secrets stayed secrets around here. But there was Ray, sitting right beside everyone else, like nothing had happened.

Out-of-control Ray wasn't here today. He wasn't going to go off the deep end over a wedding dress. That smirk proved it. He was too satisfied with himself to do anything stupid.

He could do anything he wanted, and then he could mosey on in and sit through church with all of us, and nobody would even say "boo" to him. Everyone really *was* welcome at our church, no matter what.

Do your friends despise, forsake you?
Take it to the Lord in prayer!
In his arms he'll take and shield you;
you wilt find a solace there.

Time for Special Presentation. I snapped the hymnal shut and walked forward, clutching the pink Bible to my chest like a shield. I gripped the sides of the pulpit so nobody would notice my shaking hands as I read from the highlighted verses, "The body is a unit, though it is made up of many parts; and though all its parts are many, they form one body. Now you are the body of Christ, and each one of you is a part of it."

The church was the body of Christ, and the church was the people. Scattered around the pews were the hands and the feet and the heart of God.

I swallowed hard, then grabbed my Bible and held it over my head. "Who here believes this is the word of God?"

Various "Amens" and "Yeses" and "Uh-huhs" floated up to me.

"Who believes we should live by the words in this book?"

More affirmations.

I put the Bible back down, flipped to Matthew, and through my quickly closing throat, read the other verses I'd marked. "If your right hand causes you to sin, cut it off and throw it away. It is better for you to lose one part of your body than for your whole body to go into hell."

All I had to do was give them a little nudge. These were good people. They wanted to obey the Bible. Just a little reminder and Ray would be gone. He was a gangrenous hand, and if they didn't get rid of him, the church would be infected and we'd all fall into hell.

Ray didn't have the track record I had. I grew the youth group by bringing in my friends. I started prayer groups and Bible studies. I used my summers to go on mission trips and work on service projects. All Ray did was couch hop from church member to church member and eat everyone's food. I wasn't perfect, but if anyone was judging us by our fruits, I was in the lead.

Uncomfortable stares and an awkward silence filled the church until I grabbed my Bible and wedged myself back between Angela and Ben, heart hammering away.

It'd been a mistake to get up there when I was so worked up. What kind of good Christian girl stands up behind the pulpit and demands a member's excommunication? Good Christian girls were quiet and submissive, and I'd just proven I wasn't either of those things.

As soon as I was seated, Alma stood again and invited the choir to come forward. Ray went up with them, even though I didn't remember him ever singing with the choir before. Instead of allowing Alma to lead the song they'd prepared, he stood in front of the choir and held up his own Bible. "Like Kristy said, this is the word of God..."

Blood rushed into my ears, and I didn't hear the rest. I shot out of the pew and almost tripped over Ben as I stormed down the aisle and out the main doors. How dare he say my name and hold up God's word with the same hand that popped my screen out and ripped into my magazines?

Gravel slid under my platform jellies as I paced around the parking lot. The second I jumped out of the pew, I regretted it. Stomping off like that had wrecked the whole "act normal" plan. He'd baited me, and I was stupid enough to fall for it. Now he looked like a reasonable, God-fearing man while I looked like an overly emotional, hysterical girl.

The church windows were open and the choir's song spilled out. I stopped pacing and leaned against the outside wall. If I didn't get myself under control soon, I was going to cry. I needed to calm down and go back inside and try to salvage things the best I could.

When I heard Dad start his sermon, and I was pretty sure my face wasn't bright red anymore, I slipped back inside, avoided any curious or condemning stares thrown my way, and sat back down in my pew. I leaned into Ben and grabbed his left hand. He didn't say anything, but gave my hand a squeeze.

I stayed front-facing all the way through the closing hymn, focusing on the banner someone before our time had printed out on a dot matrix.

The Purpose of This Church:
1. To Glorify Jesus Christ
2. To Make Disciples
3. To Preach the Gospel

Dad dismissed the service the same way he did every Sunday. "Go in peace."

CHAPTER FIVE

After service, I escaped into the Fellowship Hall to avoid any questions about my outburst, but the door swung open right behind me. Jackie must have jumped a pew or two to catch me so quickly. "I don't appreciate what you did in there," she said, glaring at me from beneath dark, teased bangs.

Jackie favored her father, Elmer. They had the same broad build, round face, and black hair. Ben stuck out in his family with blond hair and blue eyes. It was something he and I had in common. As the only blonde, light-eyed person in my family, I didn't quite look like I belonged either.

Ben had been a late-in-life surprise for his parents. His sister, Jackie, was the same age as my mom, which was driven home by the respect-your-elders tone she was using on me. When I kept quiet because I wasn't sure which of my actions that morning she hadn't appreciated, she added, "Ray didn't break into your house."

My heart started pounding again. "Yeah, he did."

She huffed and shook her head at me, though her stiff hair didn't stir one bit. "Why do you even think that? 'Cause your mom said so?"

Of course because my mom said so. Why wouldn't I

believe Mom over a man we all knew had some serious delusions? "He's been following me around. Like, all summer."

She scoffed at that, and didn't budge when I told her other women had noticed it and brought it up to my parents. A vision of Jackie's husband trying to reason with Ray's shaved head and crazed eyes sprang up from two years ago. The ace up my sleeve. "And he's schizophrenic. We all know what he can be like," I added, like it resolved the whole argument.

She narrowed her eyes and said he *wasn't* schizophrenic, which didn't make any sense because a hospital had committed him when I was in tenth grade. Did she think Mom and the hospital were involved in a conspiracy?

She said, "He *was* schizophrenic, but we healed him."

And I suddenly remembered who I was talking to. Here was someone who took Mom's chronic illness personally. She'd prayed for Mom, but Mom hadn't gotten any better. Jackie had plenty of faith, so if Mom hadn't received a miraculous healing, it was obviously because of some sort of sin or faith deficit on Mom's part. The possibility that sometimes illness strikes people in good standing with God wasn't possible because people in good standing with God had enough faith to move mountains and rewire brains.

She, and other members of our church, believed if a person had enough faith, they could be healed of anything. If I pushed the mental illness angle, I wouldn't get anywhere with her. If I insisted Ray hadn't been healed, then I was questioning Jackie's faith. I was questioning the faith of *everyone* who'd prayed over him, and that wasn't going to win anyone over to my side. Although, if Jackie was telling Ray he was healed and didn't need to take any pills those crackpot, atheist doctors had given him, that *would* explain a few things.

Besides, everyone wants to believe they're a good judge of character. I wasn't just accusing Ray of being a creep. By pointing my finger at Ray, I was also accusing Jackie and most of our congregation of being the kind of people who would befriend a creep. If Jackie could be so close to Ray and not recognize evil when it was right in front of her, then what did that say about her? People turn a blind eye to all sorts of horrible things, just so they can maintain the illusion that they *would have known* if something terrible had really been going on. There's a reason we're so familiar with the phrase, *But he seemed like such a nice person*.

I steered away from Ray's delusions and tried a different tactic. "Who else could it be? He's the only person following me around."

She crossed her arms. "He is *not* following you around. And if he is, can you blame him with the way you dress?"

I sure was asking for it in my buttoned-up blouse and ankle-length floral skirt. The rest of the conversation blurred out for me at this point. I hadn't slept much since Angela had found me on the steps of that church in Oklahoma.

The last thing Jackie said, though, was branded into

my brain. When I was ten, my uncle said when you experience something special you should take a minute to snap a mental picture of it. Stare really hard, close your eyes, and hold the image in your mind for a second. Then you can bring it up again anytime you want.

I must have accidentally had my mental finger on the shutter release because I have a vivid mental picture of that moment. I can see Jackie standing in front of me in her sensible and modest skirt. I know she's not tall, but she seems enormous. Little bits of sawdust float in the light from the open window to her left, where an addition on our church has been going up. She's all sharp eyes and crunchy bangs. "I don't think my brother should marry you."

That knocked the wind out of me. I'd expected to get into an argument with her over Ray, but I'd never expected her to attack my relationship with Ben. I thought she cared about me. She'd always acted like she did, and had even encouraged our relationship in the beginning.

To her I was like the big, shiny toy in the *Sears Wish Book*. I looked so perfect and fun, but a few weeks after Christmas I wasn't so shiny, and I took up too much floor space, and I didn't do all the cool things she thought I could do. She liked me before, when I led Bible studies and went on mission trips. One time, when I was fourteen, I'd heard her say, "Gosh," and I piped up all bushy-tailed with, "Oh, I don't say 'gosh' because God knows what we mean when we say that." And she'd thanked me for the reminder.

She thought I was perfect for her little brother back

then. But a while back, I'd turned my nose up at biblical courtship and wore blue jean cutoffs when I rode with Ben to the sale barn. And now I thought her friend had climbed through my window, and I'd just called out anyone in the church who wasn't interested in kicking him out. I was obviously not the kind of girl who'd make a good Christian wife.

All my sleep-deprived brain could process right then was that Jackie hated me now. Would she boycott our wedding and convince their parents it was a bad idea, and would the whole family wind up hating me? Would Ben? Would he ask me to give the ring back? Ben told me what had happened to his older brother. Elmer convinced him to break off a relationship with a girl he cared about because she was Catholic. Was accusing Ray of breaking into my bedroom worse than being Catholic?

My devastated expression must have triggered some sort of empathetic reaction because Jackie's stern face softened into something like remorse, though she didn't apologize or take anything back. I told her I had to leave before I said something I couldn't unsay, and she finally let me go.

A few minutes later, Ben and I sat on my bed. He held me as I sobbed and told him about my conversation with Jackie. When I said Jackie didn't want him to marry me, he clenched his jaw and said, "She shouldn't have said that." It was the most critical thing I'd ever heard him say about his family. After we sat in silence for a minute, he added, "She didn't have any right to say that."

When he reported back to me later, he said they'd

talked about everything over lunch at his house. Jackie said she hadn't meant it "that way," but I was pretty sure there was only one way to interpret her implied *I don't want my brother to marry someone who dresses like a whore.*

Ben's mother also told Jackie she was wrong to talk to me like that, and that gave me some hope that the whole family didn't hate me. Maybe this could be salvaged after all. Maybe if I gave it some time, the whole thing would blow over and we could move on.

If I skipped church for a couple of weeks, everything would die down. Ray had a history of leaving town for long periods of time anyway. I just had to be patient.

When one of us got worked up about something, Dad would always ask, "Are you even going to remember this five years from now?"

Five years in the future I'd be a college graduate and hopefully teaching in Pine Creek. Ben and I would be married, and we might even have a kid by then. All this nonsense would be way behind me. It'd be some story Angela or I would bring up now and then, like the time we got lost while floating the river or when the brakes went out on the car while Mom was driving down a steep grade.

"Hey, remember that time our house got broken into?"

"Yeah. That was nuts."

And we'd laugh about Old Hippie Ray and wonder what ever happened to him.

Act Normal

Mom was on the phone every day asking someone else if they'd noticed anything weird about Ray and if he'd ever been inappropriate around their daughters. I wished she'd let it go. It's inconvenient when you're trying to pretend something never happened and your mother harps on it all day, every day. She sat at our dining room table, shaking a cup of ice cubes with one hand and holding the phone in the other.

If she wasn't talking on the phone, she was tying up the phone line on the computer in the kitchen, looking up websites about stalkers.

When dad first brought a squealing modem into our home, it'd been a novelty. Look, I'm typing "hello" to someone in England, and he just said "hello" back! In 1999, we were one of the few families in town with a home computer that was connected to the Internet. A few months earlier, I'd used the Internet to do research for my senior English research paper. I'd chosen to write about the Y2K scare. After sifting through all the slow-loading survivalist websites, I was sure I knew how to deliver a breech baby if civilization collapsed. (That website even had pictures.)

I could stomach the survivalist websites, but I couldn't stomach the websites that listed each state's anti-stalking laws. It was a waste of time for Mom to do all that research. Ray wasn't a stalker. He was a home invader. A personal space invader. A thorn in my side.

But not a stalker. Only famous people had stalkers.

A few days after the break-in, I walked next door to the church to get away from the clinking ice and noisy modem. I always spent a lot of time inside the church. It was like having an extra living room, with rows and rows of couches. Sometimes I brought a book to read, or I might plunk on the piano for a little while, even though I had never really learned how to play.

The small stage and altar were on my left as I walked through the side door. Above the altar, a small wooden cross hung on the wall along with a crown of thorns. I was proud of how simple our church was. No fancy gold crucifixes or candles or any of that. We'd win a humility competition for sure.

It was a little plain for a wedding, though. Maybe we could string twinkle lights around the stage. Not two weeks before our Oklahoma trip, Ben drove me to a jewelry store and told me to pick out an engagement ring. He didn't propose because he didn't have to. We'd been together for two years. Of course we'd get married.

Christmas was my favorite holiday, and I had visions of a Christmas wedding. We could decorate the stage with poinsettias and we could hand out candles for everyone to hold, like at the candlelight Christmas Eve services I'd gone to when we lived in Indiana.

I strolled down the aisle, thinking about some chocolate dipped Oreos I'd found in one of the wedding magazines. As I passed the pew Ben and I sat in every Sunday, a flash of red caught my attention. A pair of my underwear was laid out in my pew.

Act Normal

Maybe a pair had snuck into my pocket while my jeans were in the dryer. And they fell out of my pocket when I walked into the church, and when I shut the door, maybe the draft blew them up from the floor and onto this pew, which just happened to be the pew, and the very spot on the pew, where I sat every Sunday morning. It was possible.

I grabbed them, intending to shove them into my back pocket, and a mangled photo fell out of the crotch. The overhead lights reflected off the glossy picture as I picked it up. It was one of my prom pictures. In the picture, I held a hand over my heart and smiled at a roughly cut hole where Ben's head should have been.

My mind cut out, and I froze beside my Sunday morning pew, holding a mutilated picture of the person I loved most. I didn't scream or cry or fall to my knees. I just stood there because my eyes were looking at something my brain couldn't process.

It could have been seconds or minutes or a good half hour before my brain clicked back on, but when it finally did, it lurched forward so hard it left a dent on the inside of my skull.

When had Ray stolen a pair of my underwear? Had they been in the pile of laundry he'd thrown around my room the night he broke into the house? Or had he been in the house again, without us realizing it?

What did this mean? He didn't leave any of my plain, cotton underwear. He used my one red, satin pair. Was the plan to have them sitting there for everyone to see when they came in for the next church service? *Just look at the kind of underwear this whore wears. Can you blame me?*

Was this a threat against me or against Ben? He'd cut Ben's head out, not mine. Was he capable of hurting Ben?

What should I do? I could go through the embarrassment of showing the picture and underwear to my parents and tell them where I found them, which would get them even more worked up and cause even more problems with Jackie. If I spoke up about this, would she think I made it up? Would she push harder to get Ben to break up with me? Would she convince Elmer to get on board?

I could leave the underwear in my pocket, throw the picture away, and pretend I hadn't found anything at all. Nobody but Ray and I would know. But if I kept it to myself, and something happened to Ben, that'd be on me. Could I claim to love someone and not do everything in my power to keep him safe?

CHAPTER SIX

Everything smelled like skunk the day I met Ray, which helped mask most of his always-present body odor. My eyes watered every time I carried a box from the U-Haul, through the living room, and past the back door of the parsonage, where a skunk had wedged itself behind the water heater in the mudroom, sprayed, and died.

I was fourteen, and not at all happy about moving from Oklahoma to some tiny Ozark town that didn't even show up on our road atlas. I'd hoped Broken Arrow would be our last stop, but here we were in Pine Creek unloading everything we owned for the seventh time.

Ray worked on unloading the trailer, along with several other men from Dad's new church—his first church as a pastor. Ray's long, scraggly hair and beard got in the way sometimes as he pulled boxes out of the trailer and stacked them in the middle of the gravel parking lot between the parsonage and the church. Once our two couches were unburied, he pointed to one and asked Mom, "What're you doing with this one? They won't both fit in the living room," and when she didn't offer it right away, he added, "I don't even have *one* couch."

Mom had planned to stick the second couch in the

fourth bedroom, which we were using as a den, but what could the brand new pastor's wife say to a man with no couch when he was standing in front of a good chunk of her husband's new congregation? Mom gestured toward the rattier of the pair. "I guess you could take that one."

Without so much as a thank you, Ray started dragging his new couch out of the trailer. A long-haired, brunette woman walked over to Mom, her long skirt swishing as she approached. She introduced herself with a muted, gravelly voice as Ray's wife. They didn't have any furniture to sit on, and she was excited to finally have something. I found out later they'd been raising two young sons in a shack without running water, which explained the body odor. Dad told me they were ex-hippies, but bathing in the creek didn't make them sound very "ex" to me.

A little while after Dad started pastoring the small church, most of the congregation went out to eat for lunch one Sunday. I sat beside Dad, who sat across from Ray. I eavesdropped on snippets of conversations around me, but none of it was all that interesting. Dad interrupted my eavesdropping with a nudge and said, "Did you hear what he just said?"

My attention turned to Ray, who had been going on about some missionary work in South America. He leaned forward and gave me a vivid description of how humid the jungles were down there. "Know how you take a hot shower and the moisture in the air sticks to your body, even after you turn the water off?"

I shrugged, not willing to discuss what was going on

with my fourteen-year-old body when I got out of the shower.

"It's like that in the jungle."

While I was taking Algebra II and walking a half mile down our dirt road to play basketball with Angela and our down-the-road neighbor boy, Ray's wife was on her way out. She took the boys and left right before I turned sixteen. Angela and I stepped off the bus one afternoon and saw Ray gesturing and shouting on the church lawn while Dad tried to calm him down. We went inside the house and asked Mom what was going on. She told us Ruth left, and we didn't ask for any details. It wasn't any of our business, and honestly, it didn't affect my life, so I didn't care.

As it turned out, it did affect my life because Dad started counseling Ray, which meant he was at our house more often. Sometimes he ate dinner with us, and then he and Dad took up the living room so they could talk. I couldn't watch TV those nights. There were a lot of nights when Dad was busy with Ray, Mom was busy sleeping away her chronic pain, and Angela and I hid out in her bedroom with Daniel, coming up with names for the Christian band we wanted to start, or trying to decide what role I could possibly play in that since I was basically tone-deaf.

Ray stopped by the parsonage one winter day while Angela and I were in school and Dad was out. He found my miniature fox terrier in the garage, having puppies, and carried her and the puppies inside to Mom. One puppy was stillborn, but two were still breathing. He was worried they were too cold, so he filled a saucepan with warm water and bathed each one. They were wrapped up in a towel when I got home from school. I thought it was a little miracle since I loved dogs and hadn't even known Runt was pregnant. I named the two living puppies Hope and Faith, after my favorite Bible verse.

That Sunday, Mom stood up in church and offered a praise report. She was thankful Ray had been there to save the puppies. Everyone smiled up at her and patted themselves on the backs for being such a generous community that judged people by their fruits, not by their scruffy appearance and overwhelming B.O.

Hope was dead by the time church let out. Faith died a few hours later. Ray told me the puppies were too big for my dog to carry. He said, "That's what happens when a big dog gets at a little dog."

All winter, Ray took turns sleeping at people's houses because his shack wasn't insulated well. Some nights he slept on our couch. Angela came home one day and found him lying face down in a pile of her dirty clothes. Dad explained it away by telling us Ray was prostrating himself in prayer, and she should keep her clothes off the floor anyway. But she always kept her dirty laundry in her hamper. She figured Ray must have dumped it out, but I thought he'd accidentally knocked it over. Who would dump out a girl's laundry and lie in it?

He disappeared for a few months after that. I heard some rumors he was searching for his family, and his truck had been found somewhere without him around. I wondered if he'd killed himself out of grief, and I felt bad for him, and guilty about being so annoyed about the TV during his counseling sessions.

The next time I saw Ray was on the Sunday we started having our second church service. The church was growing, and we were getting some younger families and teenagers. Dad wanted to hold a second worship service every Sunday, right after the normal service, with contemporary worship music.

On the Sunday we launched our new service, the church was packed with visitors and members. When Ray walked in, nobody recognized him. He'd shaved his head and long beard, and he didn't blink.

I had to leave early to get to a play performance, so I left the second church service about halfway through and went next door to change. As I walked out of my kitchen, Ray burst through the parsonage's front door. He stared right through me, even though I was standing in his path, took one giant side step around me, and lunged for the phone I'd been blocking.

Praise music poured from the church's open windows as I moved closer to the front door and wished for an adult. As soon as the thought popped into my head, Jackie's husband, Scott, came running out the church's side door, across the short sidewalk, and up my front steps. "What'd he do?" he asked.

"Stole our phone."

Scott walked into the house, and we both stared at Ray through the kitchen door, where he was pacing around, dragging the long phone cord, even though he wasn't talking to anyone.

A car pulled up outside, and I gave Scott what I assumed was a seriously desperate expression. "My ride's here. What do I do?"

He put a hand on my shoulder and steered me toward the front door. "I've got him. Don't worry about it."

Since Scott was a big guy, I figured he could wrestle the phone away from Ray if he had to. He was my Sunday school teacher, and he and Jackie had been our youth leaders for the past year. I trusted Scott.

I left and went to play Beth in a community theater production of *Little Women*, though my hands were still shaking when I entered from stage left. When I got home, Mom, Angela, and my friends fed me fractured accounts about what had happened next.

Scott managed to get Ray out of our house and back over to the church, but he didn't settle down. During the praise music, he leapt from his pew, started screaming in tongues, and took off running up and down the main aisle. In the midst of all the gibberish, Angela heard him shout, "I'm the devil!"

The church service ground to a halt. Dad ordered the kids outside, but Angela and our friends kept peeking in through open windows and getting shouted at for it.

While the kids stood around in the parking lot, the adults prayed over Ray. Through the prayers, Ray wouldn't let up. Some of our visitors that morning attended an Assembly of God church a few towns over. They offered to take Ray back with them and perform an exorcism. I don't know if Ray consented to that or not, but the visitors packed him up and drove away. Dad wasn't big on exorcisms, so he stayed behind while some of our other church members rode along.

A few days later, I overhead Dad tell Mom that during the ritual, Ray ran from his exorcists and jumped through a plate-glass window. They took him to a hospital where doctors stitched up his hands and diagnosed him with schizophrenia. I didn't know it then, but it wasn't the first time a hospital had admitted him for a psychotic break.

We didn't see him for a long time after that. It seemed like he was in the hospital for at least a year, but I wasn't keeping track. Maybe it was only a few months. When he came back, his hair and beard were long again, and he wasn't running around speaking in tongues or claiming to be the devil.

Some of our church members believed they'd prayed away his schizophrenia. If they had enough faith that he was harmless, God would make him harmless. And he seemed harmless. Using someone's phone without permission wasn't that big of a deal. I figured he must have had his delusions under control, or the hospital wouldn't have let him out.

Ray ignored me for the next couple of years, until we started building an addition onto the church during my senior year. Even though our church's second service never recovered after Ray's outburst, the congregation had still grown so much that we needed more room, so we were adding onto the Fellowship Hall.

A man from our church owned a portable sawmill, which he set up in our backyard. Our church members cut and stacked all the wood for the addition ourselves. There was something spiritually satisfying about a community of believers working with their hands to build a place to fellowship together.

Ray started hanging around the church more often once the walls started going up. After graduation, I quit my after-school job at Sonic so I'd have the summer before college free, so I happened to be around more often too. I did live next door to the church, after all.

He hovered around me when I'd go next door to help work on the church. Or he'd follow me from place to place at Sunday potlucks. I'd try to steer the conversation toward one of my teenage friends, but he'd hook it and try to shift my attention back to himself. I knew he must be lonely and all, but I started to get annoyed when I couldn't hang out with my friends without him constantly competing with them.

Around that time, we started getting a lot of prank calls. The phone would ring, we'd pick it up, and the person on the other end would sit there for a minute before hanging up. We shared a phone number with the church, so I figured some kids got the number out of the phone book and thought they'd have fun pestering the pastor.

Mom interrupted a movie Ben and I were watching in the living room one night and asked if Ray was bothering me. "He's annoying," I said, even though I knew the right thing to say was something more like, "Oh, heavens, no. He's one of God's children, and he can monopolize my attention all he wants."

She wasn't surprised I was annoyed. Some of the

Act Normal

newer ladies at church had noticed Ray was paying an awful lot of attention to me, and they'd asked Mom about it. "They don't think I'm *with* him, do they?" I was more alarmed anyone might think I couldn't do better than an unwashed mountain man who was as old as my dad than I was by Ray's obnoxious omnipresence.

Late that summer, Dad had a talk with Ray. He asked him to give me some more space, but it didn't do any good. He'd still march over with his own chair and wedge himself between Ben and me at church meals. The only buffer I had was my friend Garrett from church. He was several years older than I was, and maybe that made him a little more sensitive to what was going on. After Ray would squeeze in between Ben and me, Garrett would bring another chair and squeeze in between Ray and me, which always left me without enough room to maneuver my fork so I couldn't enjoy my pie.

By the time our youth group held a car wash fundraiser for our Oklahoma trip, I was thoroughly irritated with Ray. An F5 tornado had ripped through Oklahoma City that spring, and we were headed down to help Mennonite Disaster Service rebuild houses.

We had fun washing cars and raising money that morning. And then Ray showed up. He parked his truck down the street and walked over to the car wash. "When you leaving?" he asked.

More questions followed. "Who's going? When you coming back? What car you taking down?"

One of the other girls gave him some information,

but I wouldn't give him a straight answer, hoping the cold shoulder would convince him to leave. When he point-blank asked me if I was going on the trip, I won a silent staring contest with him. It wasn't any of his business whether I was going. After a while, he gave up and walked back to his truck, and I forgot all about his questions until we got that phone call in Oklahoma.

CHAPTER SEVEN

When I was ten years old, I repeated something I'd heard on some late '80s sitcom. We were driving home from the skating rink and I piped up from the backseat to ask, "When do you think I'll go through puberty?"

After a tense pause, Mom cocked her head back and told me not to use "language like that."

Eight years later, I felt more than a little awkward as I sat in a cramped sheriff's office and described my sexiest pair of underwear to Dad and the balding police officer sitting behind the desk.

Maybe I'd have been better off tossing the underwear and picture into the trash, but I was worried about Ben. Erasing a person by taking away his face was about the creepiest thing I could imagine, so I showed the picture and my underwear to my parents.

Dad drove me down to the sheriff's office to file a report about it, even though I didn't want to. I asked Dad why he couldn't go down and file it for me, but he said I had to because I was the one who found everything, and I was the "object of obsession," according to those websites Mom kept looking up to read about stalkers. That phrase was the worst. I wasn't an object.

But Ray had made me into a thing because things can be controlled.

And hadn't my own church done that to me when they quoted Romans 14:13 and told us girls to be careful about the way we dressed so we wouldn't be a "stumbling block" to our Christian brothers? A stumbling block isn't a person, made in the image of God. It's just a thing. Something you can blame for tripping you.

I didn't want to be a thing, so I sat across a desk from one of our local officers and tried to tell him what happened without sounding either too hysterical or too relaxed about it all. If I got too worked up, he'd think I was overreacting and shrug the whole thing off. If I didn't seem upset at all, well, he'd shrug that off too.

The officer listened to me, and then Dad, and nodded as we spoke. Dad wanted a restraining order, or for the police to at least warn Ray to stay away, but the police officer couldn't fulfill either of those requests. Because what real proof did we have?

Ray had driven up and down our road several times over the past few days, but that wasn't illegal. And, sure, Ray knew Dad was going to be away from home the night of the break-in, but everyone from our church knew that. Just like anyone from church knew exactly where I sat every Sunday.

Except not everyone from my church had been hanging around me all summer. And not everyone in our church had a history of delusions and violent outbursts. But that still wasn't enough proof. Besides, Ray couldn't be arrested for trying to have a conversation with me.

He hadn't been jumping through any plate-glass windows lately, and unless he publicly did something that outrageous again, people would just go right on thinking his delusions were under control.

The police officer leaned forward and rested his elbows on the desk. "If he touches you, then we can do something." He lowered his chin and raised his eyebrows on the word "touches." It was the kind of eyebrow twitch people shoot at one another when the thing they're thinking of is too vulgar to say out loud.

I shrank down into the metal folding chair, and my jaw clenched down painfully. So, all I had to do was sit tight until Ray raped me, and then the police would be all over it. Did he really think I was in *that* kind of danger? Ray was being creepy, but could someone who'd known me since I was fourteen really do *that* to me?

The police officer cleared his throat and addressed Dad. "Y'all got a gun in the house?"

I guess the officer thought Ray really *could* do that to me. I hadn't even been touched, but I felt violated. Stripped naked in that bright office. Knowing Ray had held a pair of my underwear was bad enough, but now other possibilities ran through my head. We didn't freely say the word "sex" in our house, but now I was talking to Dad and some stranger about my impending sexual assault. Because Ray forced me to talk about it.

We didn't have any guns, of course, since Dad was a Mennonite pastor. A pacifist. The Bible says, "Do not resist an evil person," and Dad lived it. At least he lived it in theory since he'd never had his theology tested before. There wasn't much religious persecution of Anabaptists in the late 1990s.

All through junior high, I'd heard about men like Dirk Willems, who'd been arrested for his Anabaptist faith. Dirk managed to escape his prison and flee across an ice-covered lake. When his jailer tried to follow, and fell through the ice, Dirk turned back to save him. He was repaid by being imprisoned again and executed. But that was all OK because Dirk's real reward was in heaven and in knowing he'd stayed true to Jesus's instructions to love your enemies. Following Christ meant laying down your life, literally, if it came down to that.

The officer was a little flustered by Dad's admission, and turned back to me. He gave me a hard, steady look and said, "Sweetheart, you need to go get yourself a bat. And you sleep with it under your bed every night."

I glanced at Dad, and forced out, "But I'm a pacifist too."

The officer closed his eyes for a second and leaned back in his chair. I expected him to spout, "God helps those who help themselves," but he didn't.

After we left the station, Dad stopped by Radio Shack to pick up a webcam. He was going to point it out the window, into the parking lot. We'd at least catch Ray on video if he skulked around the front of the house.

But last time he came around back, through my window, and we couldn't point cameras out every entrance. So, I drove myself back into town and bought a crook-handled umbrella with a big, pointy tip because the discount store didn't carry bats.

CHAPTER EIGHT

Angela upended a bottle of ketchup over her pile of mashed potatoes and looked over at Mom. "You'll be alone all day."

In a few days, Angela would start her senior year of high school, and I'd move into my dorm at UCA. That would put Mom home alone while Dad was in town at his part-time job at Radio Shack.

I picked the charred skin off my BBQ chicken. "Ray won't show up during the day. She'll be fine."

But I knew it wasn't true. He'd been driving up and down our road all week during the day, though he hadn't actually stepped foot on the property. At least we assumed he hadn't been on church property since he left my underwear and prom picture in my pew.

Angela stirred her pink mountain and glared at me. Didn't I care about what happened to Mom? Angela always got worked up about Mom and leapt to her defense. She was thirteen when Mom first started getting sick. One of the doctors had called it a "chronic illness," and Angela confused that with a terminal illness. She'd walked around for months thinking our mother was dying, and wondering why she was the only person who was upset about it before Mom figured out what her deal was and set her straight. Once you get used to that level of anxiety, it probably sticks with you, even when you know there's no reason to be so scared anymore.

"I'll call at lunch to check in," Angela said.

Dad said he'd call from work. I didn't offer to call. Ray was after me, and once I was out of the house, he'd back off. Besides, even if he did come after her, what good would a phone call do? It wasn't like Ray would hear the phone ring and suddenly realize, "Holy crap! I'm attacking the pastor's wife. What was I thinking?"

Mom finished off her Sprite and started shaking the glass of ice, dislodging a cube to chew on. As she crunched down on one, I said, "He parked by the window this morning."

Three heads popped up from their plates, and the ice cubes stopped rattling. Mom's glass banged down on the table, and she rounded on Dad. "I told you I saw his truck up by the house."

I'd skipped church that morning to avoid Ray. I hadn't missed a Sunday service in over two years, but I was sure God would understand this time. It was strange and lonely to sit on my couch and look out my lace-covered windows as the rest of the congregation pulled into the parking lot and walked into church without me.

Our church welcomed everyone, which sounded like the sort of loving policy a bunch of Christians should have, but what that really meant was everyone was welcome *except* me. Because if Ray was there, I couldn't be. Predator and prey can't sit in the same room together.

Dad had approached the church council after we

talked to the police officer. He wanted the council members to intervene and ask Ray to temporarily attend a different church for a while. That way I could still attend without running into Ray every Sunday morning. The church council members refused to ask him. Elmer didn't think it was fair to Ray. If I wasn't willing to pretend everything was normal, it was easier on the church if I just stopped coming. If I kept quiet and out of sight, none of the church council members would have to do anything.

As I watched out my window that Sunday morning, Ray's truck had pulled up right beside the window nearest the couch where I was sitting. He'd had to pull halfway into our front yard to get that close. I turned away and stared into the kitchen as he got out, so at least he wouldn't have the satisfaction of making eye contact. Once I was sure he'd had enough time to strut over to the church (across an entire parking lot that could have accommodated his truck), I turned back toward the window, and he was gone.

Mom glared at her plate as Dad suggested maybe he couldn't find a better spot. Of course, nobody ever parked up in our yard when there was a parking lot and a whole dirt road out front they could park along. But it'd have been a lot easier if he couldn't have found a better spot, and I didn't blame him for wishing it. Mom sure blamed him for wishing it, though.

She said Dad never noticed anything, like how he never noticed all those times Ray cornered me at church, and if he had, he could have dealt with it right when it started. He wanted to know how he was supposed to notice everything that every person did during a potluck. Angela narrowed her eyes at me for starting the fight, so I just ate my chicken, and in the end, Dad told me not to sit in the living room on Sunday mornings.

So, I couldn't attend the church I'd been a part of for four years, and now I couldn't even sit in my own living room on Sunday mornings.

I wanted to pop off with some sarcastic comment, but I didn't because Angela wouldn't have been all worried, and Mom and Dad wouldn't have fought if I hadn't gone and gotten myself stalked.

That's what Mom's web searching called it. *Stalking.* I thought only famous people had stalkers, but maybe a pastor's daughter counted as famous in a small church.

Mom had a whole slew of bookmarked websites. They listed all the creepy things any stalker had ever done, but no list was ever complete because some stalker out there would always see terrorizing someone as a creative challenge and come up with a new idea.

My parents ticked Ray's behaviors off the generic lists they found:

Trying to monopolize my attention
Following me
Driving past the house
Leaving "gifts"
Calling and hanging up

He was definitely a stalker, even if I had a hard time wrapping my head around the term.

I also couldn't wrap my head around the *why*. Why me? Ben and I had been together for almost two years, and we were engaged, so I wasn't available. Compared to my sister, with her dark hair and eyes, much better nose-to-face ratio, and charismatic personality, I wasn't even the most attractive girl in our church. What had I done to invite that sort of attention? And what could I do to un-invite it?

Our biggest challenge was the law. Arkansas had passed an anti-stalking law a few years back, but it was almost impossible to arrest anyone under it. We had to prove that Ray was the person who broke into our house. Ray was the person leaving creepy things for me to find. And, most importantly, Ray was dangerous. If we couldn't prove he was dangerous and I was afraid for my life, he couldn't be arrested for stalking me. Phone hang-ups and creepy gifts were inconvenient, but were they *dangerous*? Could I really say I was afraid for my life?

I had a hard time believing that a man—even a clearly delusional man—who had known me for so long would hurt me. Maybe he was just in the middle of another one of his breakdowns and it'd burn out soon.

We couldn't force him to stop. The police couldn't force him to stop. Whether or not it all stopped tomorrow or dragged on forever was up to Ray. He was the only one in control.

CHAPTER NINE

The first time Ben kissed me, he said he was sorry. He drove me home from the youth rally that night and parked between the parsonage and church. We talked for a while, just like we always did. In a few minutes, I'd be out past curfew. I was tired, so I let my head fall back against the truck seat and shut my eyes while he continued a now one-sided conversation.

I floated down into that halfway stage of sleep, where you aren't quite awake and you aren't quite asleep. In my almost-dream, Ben kissed me. Except it wasn't a dream. Ben had snuck up on me while my eyes were closed.

I froze. At first I wasn't convinced it was actually happening, and by the time I decided Ben really *was* kissing me, I wasn't sure if it was wise to suddenly make a move after being still for so long. Any movement and he might come to his senses and realize who it was he was kissing in the cab of his truck and recoil in horror. And I'd never kissed anyone before. There had to be some right and wrong ways of going about it, but heck if I knew what they were.

Boys hardly ever paid any attention to me, so Ben's interest was downright miraculous. We'd met two years before when my family first drove from Oklahoma to

Arkansas to visit the church. We spent the night at Ben's house, and I met him a few minutes before we all left for church the next morning. He sat in silence beside me on his parents' couch and didn't even glance my way to say "hello." But he was a senior and I was a gawky freshman, so what'd I really expect?

He warmed up to me on a Mennonite Disaster Service trip, about a year later. While sitting through a church service, he saw me laugh, tap my friend on the shoulder, and point out the words "do not covet thy neighbor's ass" in the bulletin. This blue-eyed, nineteen-year-old boy, who'd never slung more than a couple of words my way, walked up to me after the service, smiled, and whispered in my ear. "Stop coveting Nick's ass, Kristy."

His girlfriend broke up with him as my junior year started. I heard he wasn't in good shape, so I called to see if he needed anyone to talk to. He came over, and we sat on my parents' couch for hours. I didn't know much about breakups, so I mostly listened. He came over a second night, and when he went to leave I handed him a poorly constructed poem I'd written for him in pink gel ink. "One day you will awaken and the pain will be gone," it said, because I was sixteen and didn't know what I was talking about.

That fall, I became something like a confessor for him. He whispered secrets to me in the back of vans on youth trips or while sitting on my living room couch. He'd tell me what he'd done and who he'd done it with, and no matter how shocked I was or how ill-equipped I was to handle what he told me, I'd smile, place a steady hand on his back, and tell him it was OK. My acceptance absolved him of even the imagined sins that weren't his fault, but weighed on him. I felt like we understood one another. I may not have done the things he'd done, but I did understand the pressure to live up to what was expected of you. I knew what it felt like to know that every choice we made reflected back on our fathers and their roles in the church. But Ben took it to heart in ways I never did.

As soon as I realized Ben definitely *was* kissing me, I thought about God, which sounds like an odd thing to think about when you're finally experiencing your first kiss, but my entire life was saturated with God. Prayer meetings and Bible studies and service projects. Ben and I had met because of Dad's call to ministry. We'd gotten to know one another on youth group trips. Everything between us had started in our church—had started with God. So, of course I thought about God.

My now fully awake brain was running full speed when Ben pulled away and stared at me in the not-so-flattering dashboard light. "Sorry," he whispered.

"For what?"

I expected him to say he was caught up in the moment or he was lonely—some kind of lame, but believable excuse that would let me down easy.

He shifted to move back into his own seat and faced the windshield. "I'm sure you weren't expecting that," he said.

It didn't sound like the prelude to a *you are the worst*

kisser in the world, let's just be friends speech, but he wasn't handing me his class ring either. "What do you mean?" I asked.

An uncharacteristic avalanche of words spilled out of his mouth. "I don't know if you know I like you. Maybe you weren't expecting me to do that, and now you're sitting here like, Whoa. What's this?"

Now I was a little offended. *What's this?* I might not have had boys falling all over me, but I knew what a kiss meant.

I stared at him without saying anything for a minute. He knew I'd only had one boyfriend, and he was a long-distance boyfriend I'd only seen in person once. Maybe that didn't even count. I thought he was worried about pushing me into more than I was ready for, but then I remembered I hadn't kissed him back, and maybe he didn't know I was asleep when he'd moved in. Maybe he thought I didn't want him.

I wasn't sure what to say. My first instinct, as usual in an awkward situation, was to make a joke. Tease him a little. But he was sitting there all tense-necked, staring out the window, waiting for me. I'd tagged along with Ben since the school year had started, devouring any scrap of attention he threw my way. Now he was waiting for *my* attention. One kiss, and suddenly I wasn't the tagalong kid anymore. One kiss, and I was in control of what happened next. I'd never had that much power over another person before, and I couldn't decide if I liked it or not.

My fingertips touched his arm, and he turned his

head. "I thought it was pretty obvious we liked each other," I said.

He gave me a tiny smile that made my chest thump. I wanted to lean over and give this kissing thing another go, but didn't want to look like *that* kind of girl. I wouldn't have the chance anyway because the porch light flashed. I was out past curfew, and Dad wasn't happy.

I slid out of the truck seat, but before I shut the door, I decided to drop something really mature and wise-sounding on him, just to drive home how not-a-kid I was. "You don't have to worry about me. I'm pretty tough." I smiled and added, "I won't break."

Two years later, Ben and I walked hand-in-hand through kitschy shops at Silver Dollar City. It was our last trip to Branson before my semester at UCA started. I hadn't slept well since the break-in, and I felt it. I'd grabbed a nap on the way up, but walking around in the late-summer heat had sapped whatever energy that had given me.

The silent drive up had been for the best. I was a dog with a bone, and Ben was tired of listening to me go over and over the recent events. At the drive-in two nights ago, I'd talked over the crackling speaker hanging off Ben's window. Elmer's idea that Ben's ex-girlfriend might be stalking me was insane, I told him. He thought she was jealous about our engagement, but Rachel had broken up with Ben. Besides, she and I got along fine. She even braided my hair in English class, and you don't just braid a girl's hair and then steal her underwear.

Elmer's second guess was as ridiculous as his first. Our old youth group leader's son, Nick, had a little crush on me a couple of years back. Elmer asked if I thought it was possible Nick was jealous and left the prom picture in my pew. Nick was one of the nicest people I knew, and our friendship had ended because of some stupidity on my part, not because of anything he'd done. I went off on a marathon-length rant against that suggestion. Why was Elmer picking on everyone except the one man who was actually creepy?

Ben's silence wore on me until I boiled over and demanded he say *something*.

He responded with a drawn out sigh. "What do you want me to say?"

He sounded so exhausted, and honestly, I didn't know what I wanted him to say. Some part of me thought if he took it all more seriously, I might be able to take it less seriously. Share the burden a little.

Ray had been a third wheel for the past couple of weeks, but this was supposed to be a nice trip. We needed a break, so I wouldn't bring any of it up. This would be a normal day.

It was muggy out, and I was content to stand around in the shop's air conditioning for as long as he wanted to browse. He headed toward a table of old-fashioned magic tricks and tugged me right along.

"Know how this one works?" He held up a pair of horseshoes that were attached with a chain, with a third horseshoe around the middle chain. They looked like handcuffs, and I said so.

He slipped the two horseshoes over my wrists. *Oh, really?* my jumping eyebrow said. He smirked and raised his eyebrows back at me, and I could almost pretend everything *was* normal.

I took the cuffs off and fiddled with the trick for a while. Ben was ready to move on, but I wasn't going to be beaten by some stupid horseshoes. I pulled at the third piece of metal, but I couldn't figure it out.

Ben wrapped his arm around my waist and leaned in. "I'll buy it and show you how it works if you'll wear them until we leave."

"Why would I walk around with my hands tied together?"

He shook his head, and seemed embarrassed he'd even brought it up, but explained anyway. "I mean one on you and one on me. It'd be cute?"

I told him to buy it. Who cared if amusement park strangers thought we were a couple of freaks with a handcuff fetish? I wasn't ever going to see any of these people again, anyway.

We walked through the rest of the shops linked together. The horseshoe was heavy and banged against my bony wrist. I laced my fingers through his to keep some of the pressure off. It was a lot less comfortable than it'd sounded in the shop, but I didn't pull my hand out until we got to the car and he showed me how to turn the chain and remove the third horseshoe.

As we drove home, we took up our normal positions, with me scooched over as close to him as possible. "Did your dad say anything about the rock house?" I asked.

Ben's parents owned a vacant house. It'd belonged to Ben's grandparents and hadn't been used in years. Elmer had given us permission to live there after we got married, but Jackie had recently popped up and said she planned to move back to Pine Creek and live there.

I'd challenged her at the dinner table a few days before the Oklahoma trip. It wasn't fair of her to yank the house out from under us. She was the same age as my mother, and she'd had time to save up to buy or rent a place. Besides, she and Scott already owned a house an hour outside Pine Creek. Ben and I, on the other hand, would be starting out with nothing.

Jackie said we could wait longer to get married or Ben and I could always move in with his parents for a while. Over the past couple of days, I'd started to suspect her comments about not wanting her brother to marry me were more motivated by her housing situation than the Ray situation.

Ben tensed up. "Well, I've been thinking about that whole deal. We could stay in the basement until we get our own place."

He'd been living in his parents' basement since I'd met him. Now he expected a wife to join him down there with the little lizard that seemed to live in his shower. My back jerked straight. "There is no way I'm living with your parents."

He wanted to know why.

I lectured him on what marriage was, or at least what I thought it was. The Bible said two people were supposed to leave their parents to make a new family. How could you form a new family when you were still living with your old family?

He'd walked me through the rock house that summer, and I had ideas about fixing it up. All I'd ever wanted was a stable home. When I was married and settled in my own home, I'd never be jerked across state lines again. I could finally put down roots and feel like I was part of a real community.

Ben and I weren't speaking the same language. He'd only ever lived in Pine Creek. His father had grown up in Pine Creek. His grandfather was from Pine Creek. I suppose when you've got such deep roots, it's hard to understand why someone else might be desperate for a tiny corner of your garden. I'd spent most of my life in rental houses and a parsonage that might as well have been a rental. I wanted a real home. I wanted to sew up some curtains (I could learn how to sew) and cook dinner for him every night (I could learn how to cook). Those things couldn't happen in his parents' basement.

We went back and forth for a while. I drew lines in the sand I didn't mean, and he stepped right over them because he knew he could. He never raised his voice (I did), but there was no budging him on it. Jackie would get the house. He was staying in the basement.

When I couldn't persuade him, I rocketed over to the passenger side, cranked up the radio, and gave him the silent treatment all the way home. Instead of turning down the dirt road to the parsonage when we got back, he drove past the turnoff and took another dirt road, which led to another, which led to a field hidden behind a screen of trees along the road. He parked behind the trees, shut the truck off, and turned to stare at me until I gave up and turned back. We stared at one another for a while. "I love you," he finally said. He didn't say it out loud, but trailing on those words was, "Isn't that enough?"

We did love one another. I'd never cared about anyone the way I cared about him. Even though I was still irritated, I inched closer and wrapped both arms around his neck. He kissed me and pulled me across the truck seat until I was halfway on his lap.

The windows were still rolled up, and it was hard to breathe, but I didn't want to stop long enough to roll them down. If we stopped, we'd fight again. Right now, everything was OK. All the frightening things that'd happened were background noise, and the only parts of my life in focus were his mouth, his hands. Now I was safe. I was wanted. I was loved.

A while later, he was still catching his breath when I wrapped my fingers around the back of his neck and whispered, "I'll live in the basement. I'll live anywhere."

He didn't reply, but clutched at me like I'd threatened to leave instead of given in. But I'd given in almost immediately. I could survive living with my in-laws as long as someone loved me this much, and anyway, love always requires some sacrifices.

CHAPTER TEN

The sweet aftertaste of cigar paper stuck to my lips as I passed the blunt to Olivia. It'd gone around the circle several times, passing me over because I'd been our high school's *See You at the Pole* girl and the *let's perform a skit about how rotten drugs are* girl, until I reached out, took it from Sara, and asked, "How? Like a cigarette?"

Yeah, they said, like a cigarette.

I held the smoke in my mouth and allowed a little to trickle down my throat and into my lungs before letting the fog roll back out of me. My church definitely would not approve. *Look how far she's fallen. Drugs. Can you believe it? What's next, prostitution?*

Round and round we went as candied smoke twirled up and hit the ceiling in Erin's living room. I inhaled giant middle fingers and blew them back out at everyone who thought they had the right to tell me what to do. Tonight, I was the only person in charge of me.

It was a rebellious impulse, and maybe I'd have done it anyway once I was out of my parents' house and I didn't have to worry about curfews and rules. Or maybe I only went out with Olivia that night because I was too scared to stay in my dorm room alone. Maybe, if everything had been normal, I would have stayed at the dorm and done my homework.

Christians are supposed to be strong in the face of adversity, and I had been. For a whole four days. I'd sat in my dorm room those nights, pink Bible on my lap, licking my fingers and flipping through the tissue-thin pages looking for *something*. Some answer. Some comfort. Some way out.

The best I'd come up with was James 1:2, which I underlined so I wouldn't forget.

Consider it pure joy, my brothers, whenever you face trials of many kinds, because you know that the testing of your faith develops perseverance.

That night, I'd prayed for perseverance. My faith was being tested, but it'd ultimately make me stronger. I could get through this. If God was for me, who could be against me?

I'd planned to go home Thursday night after my last class, but when I called Mom to see what time she was coming to pick me up, she told me she wasn't coming at all. Ray had left something in the mailbox, and she didn't want to tell me what it was at first, but I hounded her. It was a picture of a bride. He tore it out of a wedding magazine, wrote MINE across the bride's chest in black marker, and left it in our mailbox.

Mom thought it meant he planned to kidnap me. She thought it was safer for me to stay on campus, even though I thought it was better for me to be home, near my friends and Ben, because it'd been a rough first week of college and I wanted to be somewhere comfortable and familiar.

I've never been great at handling change. All my life, people have accused me of being overly sensitive. Moving out of my parents' house and starting college while having to adjust to a stalker was a little bit too much for me. I might have been physically safer on campus, but I felt emotionally safer at home.

When I was alone, I couldn't distract myself from thinking about Ray, which was exactly what he wanted. As more "gifts" showed up at the house, I started to think Ray believed I wanted to be with him. When a note arrived warning my family not to get in the way of what was his, I was even more convinced. These weren't messages for me. They were messages for my parents. *She's mine. Get out of our way and let us be together.* The prom picture could've been a similar message directed not at me, but at Ben. If he wasn't sending messages directly to me, to try to convince me that we should be together, he must have thought I was already on board. Thoughts like that kept my appetite suppressed.

I was scared, and I was sad, and I was exhausted because no matter how tired I was, I couldn't sleep. And I was lonely out here, isolated from my family and from Ben.

I wanted to do just about anything to avoid having to sit around puzzling out Ray's delusions. So, I stuck close to Olivia and Sara, who'd always been nice to me in high school, and they stuck close to some apartments in town where other former schoolmates lived. One apartment was full of girls who'd graduated high school the year before us, and the other apartment was full of boys from our graduating class. I wasn't particularly close to any of those people, but they didn't seem to mind me hanging around, and at least I was around people I knew.

I just wanted to go home, though. Some kids can't wait to get out of their hometown when they graduate, but I wasn't one of those kids.

When I got offered the scholarship from UCA, I decided Conway was close enough to Pine Creek that I could commute if I wanted. Or I could stay in the dorm a couple of days a week and spend the other nights at home, which would give me plenty of time with Ben most evenings. But now my plans had gone to crap, and I had to make it two solid weeks on campus, and God only knew when I'd get to go home after that.

But I stopped thinking about all that on Erin's couch. My overactive brain settled down and broadcast white static. No Ray. No Jackie or Elmer or Mom or Dad or Ben. Thoughts flitted from nothing in particular to nothing that mattered to nothing at all.

I listened to the voices around me and watched the smoke rise and licked my lips. And when we drove back to campus, I thought the sign for Schmidt Hall said Shit Hall, and I laughed so hard I started to hyperventilate, and I slept all night without a single nightmare.

CHAPTER ELEVEN

Mom stood in the parking lot, talking to someone. It was probably our youth group leader, Travis. Angela called him Uncle T when she wanted to tease him. One time, she pulled up next to his police car at the stoplight and tried to get him to race her when it turned green, but he just wagged his finger at her. When she got to school, he pulled in after her and told her not to be such a speed demon through town.

Angela and I would show up at his house around dinner sometimes because he'd always offer to feed us. We'd sit and talk to his wife and hold their new baby. It felt like having an aunt and uncle.

Travis was at the house a lot lately. Mom called him when something new showed up because he took it more seriously than the sheriff's department. Even though he worked for the town's police department, and we were technically just outside town limits, he was trying to get some solid evidence.

Ray had been leaving pages of scripture ripped out of a Bible. He underlined some of the verses in red ink, but it didn't make any sense. He called me a sorcerer, and he seemed obsessed with Leviticus and Ezekiel. A week earlier, I noticed a verse on one of the pages was highlighted in yellow. It was a verse I thought I'd highlighted a long time ago when I was trying to memorize some Sunday school verses when I was in junior high. I checked the bookshelf in the hall, but my red NIV Bible was gone. I asked Angela to get hers since she had the same one. When we checked the page number of the ripped out page against her intact page, the verses all matched up.

Ray had stolen my Bible and my underwear. Maybe he'd done it on the same night.

I stepped out of Olivia's backseat and smiled at whatever person Mom was talking to. They tilted a little, but I was pretty sure nobody noticed I was high. Then the front steps were under me, and I was inside.

Ben was waiting in the living room, watching *Scooby Doo*, and that was the most hilarious thing that'd happened to me all week. I laughed all the way to my bedroom, but he didn't understand why it was funny.

He was worried because I seemed off. We didn't have any secrets, and I wasn't ashamed or anything, so I told him we'd passed a joint around the car on the way home. It helped take the edge off because I never knew what I'd come home to.

"You shouldn't be doing that," he said.

"We shouldn't do a lot of things we do."

I knew that would shut him up since it wasn't like he was going to keep his hands off me. He never did. And he didn't have to because Dad was at work and Angela was at school and Mom was out front talking to probably-Travis, and I missed him so much, and as soon as I kissed his neck, he dropped it.

Racetracks usually aren't the best places to study, but I was getting more done on that wobbly, wooden bench than I'd gotten done all week. Cars buzzed past as I read a section in my philosophy textbook about euthanasia. I needed to get caught up, but it was my first weekend home in two weeks, and there was no way I was staying in my room to study instead of going out with Ben. So, I sat in the front row, beside Ben, and watched the race between pages I read by the floodlights pointed down at the dirt track.

The pot had worn off a little after I got home the night before, and I hadn't slept. Between the monotonous buzzing of the cars and the monotonous British professor's voice I read the text in, my eyes were starting to glaze over. After reading the same paragraph several times without a single word sinking in, I gave up. I stacked three thick books beside Ben and lay across the bench with my head propped up on about $600 worth of textbooks. Ben reached down and ran his fingers through my hair, and I closed my eyes.

The cars were kind of soothing. A constant roar that got closer and farther away, but still blocked everything else out like white noise. I could relax here, surrounded by people. Ben was with me. Daniel's parents and sister sat two benches away. This was a safe place.

"You need to get her home, Ben."

I opened my eyes to the upside-down face of Daniel's older sister. "You sick?" she asked.

I sat up and smiled. "She's fine," Ben said, grabbing my knee and giving it an affectionate little shake.

She glanced down at the stack of books. "Studying too hard?"

"You know me. Always with the—" I tapped my index finger against my head.

She laughed, then walked back to her family. Ben wrapped his arm around me and leaned forward as one of his favorites advanced a spot. He watched the race, I watched him, clouds of dust spun off the track, and the cars went round and round because there was nowhere else to go.

CHAPTER TWELVE

I was stone-cold sober the next time I came home for the weekend, so I know for sure Mom was talking to Travis when I walked into the house. They sat at the dining room table, and Travis said something about fingerprints.

That perked my ears right up, so I took a seat beside him and went to move the Sprite can that was sitting in front of me when Mom jumped halfway out of her chair and shouted, "Don't touch that!"

I jerked my hand back and got ready to tell her off for being so greedy about her Sprite when Travis turned to me and said, "It's evidence."

My parents and Angela had left the house that morning. When they got back, Angela opened the fridge and saw everything in it had been moved around.

"Moved around?" I asked. "How could she even tell?" It wasn't like we kept a chart hanging on the wall beside the fridge. Eggs go here. Milk goes here.

But it hadn't just been rearranged. Everything was shoved to the back wall and neatly stacked so there was plenty of empty space in the front half of the fridge, and an open Sprite can sat right in the middle of the empty space, even though nobody had opened a can and left it in the fridge.

Ray had broken into the house again.

Moving ketchup and expired yogurt around sounds like a pretty lame thing for a stalker to do, but it's not. Because it's not about making someone hunt one extra second for what they went to the fridge to get. It's the message that's important. *I was here. I can get to you any time I want, and there's nothing you can do to stop me.*

And it was clever. He could have trashed the living room, but he didn't. He messed around with the fridge because who would take people seriously if they went around complaining that someone broke into their house and moved their cheese singles? *We'd* look like the crazy ones if we did that.

Ray had also delivered some more paperwork for me. A picture of another bride from my wedding magazine. This one was a blonde in a strapless, white, overly ruffled dress. He scratched her face out with black ink.

Travis understood the message and took it seriously, even if he wasn't "officially" handling the case and was technically outside his jurisdiction here. He pulled out a plastic bag and sealed the can inside so he could send it to a lab and see if they could pull any fingerprints off it. Hopefully, Ray hadn't worn gloves, and hopefully, the condensation on the can hadn't ruined any potential fingerprints.

That can was the best news we'd had in weeks. Travis tried his best not to get my hopes up, but they bubbled up anyway. If we had his fingerprints, he couldn't deny being in the house. How on earth would he justify being in our house when we kept telling the police we didn't want him there? They'd find the prints. They'd arrest him. And I could get on with my life.

It took me two days to get a hold of Ben. Even then, I had to drive to his dad's pole barn and talk to him while he welded and I stood facing the wall so the sparks wouldn't melt my eyes out of my head.

My shadow on the wall darkened every time he bent down to join metal. Every once in a while, he'd stop and lift his face shield long enough to say a sentence, then flip it back down, metal arcing and popping over whatever I said back to him.

I told him about the Sprite can, but he was confused by that since Mom drank Sprite.

"Not the point. It wasn't her can."

But he thought maybe she left it there and forgot. Who keeps track of every can they drink out of?

"Everything in the fridge was moved around. And she doesn't drink straight from the can. She says it tastes like metal."

His large shadow paused on the wall, but he didn't reply.

"You think she made it up?" I asked.

He set down his equipment, and I turned to face him. "She takes a lot of pills," he said.

She took muscle relaxers and acid reducers, but nothing that would cause her to invent a stalker. And what about my window screen? *Someone* had climbed through my window that night. How could Mom have done it when half the time she needed help walking across the hall to get to the bathroom? And why would she leave me a picture with Ben's face cut out? Or the pictures of brides?

"Maybe it's some kind of a mental breakdown."

That was the rumor going around church. According to Jackie, for some reason (possibly, a demonic reason), Mom had snapped. She was going around leaving magazine brides and cut-up pictures and sneaking through windows and throwing laundry and stealing her daughter's underwear and blaming it all on Ray, even though Mom wasn't the person following me around at potlucks or driving by the parsonage all day.

Even if Jackie honestly did believe Mom was behind everything, it didn't make sense. If anyone really thought that, why hadn't they contacted me to say, "Hey, we're worried about you coming home on the weekends to your crazy mother. How about you crash on my couch when you come home until all this gets settled?" If they thought Mom was guilty, why were they letting me walk into that house? Because when you got right down to it, what difference did it make *who* was doing these things to me? *Someone* was. Being in that house put me in some level of danger, no matter who was scratching out faces.

Maybe Jackie and her church friends did believe it was Mom. Maybe they prayed every night for her to come back to reality and stop hurting me. Or maybe Mom was just a convenient scapegoat who could take the heat off Ray. Maybe they were using her to cast enough doubt on the situation to keep Ray out of trouble. It was possible Ray put the idea into Jackie's head to begin with, telling her my parents hated him and were out to get him, and Jackie didn't understand enough about paranoid delusions to know one when she heard it.

It would sure be easier for Ben if it was Mom. Because then I'd have to make a choice, and that would be an easy choice. Ben's family or my delusional stalker of a mother? I'd pick Ben's family, of course, and I'd apologize to Ray for believing Mom, and he'd say he understood. Jackie would gloat for a while about how right she'd been, and I'd be all humble about being wrong, and we'd make up, and I'd be folded into the family, and everything would go back to normal. It'd go back to normal for Ben, at least. I'd have to cut off my family.

But if Ben admitted it was Ray, *he* would have to make a choice. Fall in line with the claims his sister was making about Mom (claims his father hadn't rebuked) or stand behind me. It wasn't such an easy choice.

A few months earlier, I'd already made him choose. He was voted in as the church's youth leader at the beginning of the year. As the months went by, fewer and fewer kids showed up for our Thursday night youth group meetings. When I asked around to find out why, most of the kids gave me the same answer. They weren't comfortable with Ben leading the group. He was too close to the rest of us in age, and it was weird since he and I were together. And some of them knew we "did some stuff," so how could they take him seriously when he taught Sunday school and talked about self-control?

They had a point. I sat Ben down in my bedroom one Saturday night and discussed it with him. I was worried we were going to turn our friends away from God. If they stopped coming to youth group and Sunday service, how could they stay right with God? Even though I didn't think the things we did were that big of a deal, I didn't want to get in the way of other kids' spiritual development. Either we should knock it off and stick to a strict discipline of celibacy, or Ben should resign and let someone else take over.

He wasn't sure how it'd look if he stepped down, and I asked, "What do you care about more? How you look to all them?" I shoved my hand toward the general direction of the church, "Or how you look to God? You need to figure out what's right and do it."

A week later, without warning me ahead of time, he raised his hand during Sunday morning announcements and said, "I'm gonna have to step down as youth leader for now."

I was prouder of him than I'd ever been. I don't remember how Dad responded to his announcement. What I do remember is twisting my head around to rubberneck past Ben, across the main aisle to where his parents sat. If I was a little surprised he'd gone ahead and stepped down, that was nothing compared to the shock I read on Elmer's red face. Ben obviously hadn't talked to his father about stepping down before he did it. He probably figured Elmer would talk him out of it, and I gave Ben a lot of credit for realizing that and having the guts to go over his father's head like that.

Now he had to choose again because that's how life works. A life doesn't spin around one single right or wrong decision. Those kinds of decisions fly at your face nonstop. We don't get a break from morality, and we wouldn't be getting a break from Ray either.

CHAPTER THIRTEEN

I was still high when Olivia dropped me off at the dorm. My key punched into the lock, and scraped tumblers echoed down the empty hall. I locked the door behind me, peeked into both closets, and checked under the bunk bed. I even looked under the desks, just to make sure.

I sat down on the bottom bunk and clicked the TV remote. Quippy one-liners bounced off white cinder block walls.

I needed to pee—bad—but I didn't get up.

The bathroom was down the hall, and with a jolt, I *knew* Ray was standing in the hall, waiting for me right on the other side of the door.

Blood pounded in my ears, and I couldn't catch my breath. My eyes darted to the door, and I launched myself off the bed, shoulder straight into the door to make sure it was really locked. It was.

I was safe in this room. And I was high. And I needed to pee. And Ray was waiting for me. If I left my room, he would grab me, and I'd be his, and he'd scratch my face out.

Another door opened in the hall, and I heard muffled voices as a group of students walked past my room.

A herd. I'd be safe in a herd.

I flung my door open. Ray wasn't on the other side, but I could still feel him there, watching me. I *always* felt him watching me.

I speed-walked down to the bathroom before the other students could make it to the stairs and disappear.

The bathroom was empty. I jumped into a stall and peed faster than I'd ever peed before.

But now I was stuck again. Because I knew he was out there waiting for me.

What if he came into the bathroom? I'd be trapped in this stall.

The gray walls tilted toward me.

When I was younger, I saw a woman on *Oprah*. A man had kidnapped her and kept her in a box for years.

What if he stole my face and put me in a box?

What if he kept me like a pet in a box in his shack in the woods?

What would happen when winter rolled around? He'd start sleeping on different church member's couches, and I'd starve. When spring came, he'd bury the box in the woods and nobody would know I was there.

And hundreds of years later someone would build a house there, and they'd accidentally dig me up, and they'd call me the Mysterious Girl in the Box because they wouldn't know my name or how I got there.

They won't know my name. I won't ever have existed if they don't know my name. I'll be nothing.

I'm nothing.
I can't breathe.
I'm trapped in a box.

The main bathroom door opened, and two girls walked in, chatting. I didn't even flush, but yanked up my pants and left the stall. The hallway blocks grew and shrank as I ran back to my room with a key in my hand so I could stab Ray in the eye if I had to. I didn't care if I looked crazy because obviously I *was* crazy.

I jabbed my key into the doorknob and leapt into the room like a kid who turns off the light, then runs and jumps into bed so a monster won't stick its claw out from beneath the bed and grab her ankle.

Before I sat back down on my bed, I rechecked both closets, under the bed, and under the desks. Because I *always* had to make sure.

CHAPTER FOURTEEN

The leather chair squeaked as I leaned forward, elbows on knees, and stared at the middle-aged man and his notepad. "I'll tell you everything," I said, "and then you tell me, on a scale from one to ten, just how crazy I am."

He raised his eyebrows, but didn't take the bait, so I plowed ahead with my tale of woe. I figured the quicker I vomited the information up, the quicker I could be done with the whole thing.

A counseling session hadn't been *my* idea. Mom had forcefully marched me into this suit-wearing man's office that morning.

Perfectly spaced vertical blinds let in skinny poles of sunshine that spread across my shoes. He didn't interrupt as I laid it all out, flat-toned like I was telling him a story about someone else.

"I'm being stalked by a schizophrenic middle-aged man I go to church with. He hasn't even touched me, but I can't sleep, and I'm skipping classes, and I can't even go to the bathroom by myself at night without freaking out."

I risked getting busted and told him how I'd been using pot to relax. I even dipped into any sort of drama from my childhood I could dredge up, and all but triple-dog-dared him to say I was sane.

When I was done, he took a deep breath and began calmly with, "First of all, you're not crazy."

I wanted to kick his chair out from under him. "Normal people don't act like this," I cut in.

Lately, I'd been skipping most of my classes and surviving on pizzas from the only place that would deliver to my dorm room. Every time I left my room, I wondered if I'd run into Ray. He didn't know what building I lived in, but he knew where my campus was. Even if he hadn't seen the scholarship letter on my wall, he'd have heard me talking about it in church. Heck, my scholarship announcement had been in the newspaper. Ray knew exactly where I was. All he had to do was walk around campus for a couple of days until he spotted me, then follow me back to my room. But if I didn't leave my room, he wouldn't have the chance.

He said normal people did act like that when dealing with "prolonged traumatic stress." They avoid what they're afraid of, like running into a stalker while walking around campus. And they get angry, which is what happens when you're stripped of control. It was even more complicated for me because I was at the age when most people get to experience the freedom to make their own decisions for the first time, but Ray's actions and my parents' attempts to protect me had robbed me of that newly earned independence. So, it was natural I'd rebel a little against my strict, religious upbringing to compensate.

He went on about fight-or-flight responses and how damaging it could be when that response was being triggered repeatedly. He said panic attacks were normal in situations like mine, and I argued that the bathroom incident wasn't a panic attack, even though it totally was. I couldn't call it that, though. I didn't want to be the kind of person who would panic in a crisis. I never had been that kind of person.

When I asked him what advice he could give me about dealing with Ray, he redirected and asked me about my feelings, which was a useless topic. I didn't need to sit around talking about my feelings. How would that stop Ray? I could barely register any emotions beyond anger and anxiety, anyway. If I thought too hard about it, or tried to touch on anything other than how angry I was, it was overwhelming. I was in survival mode, so I didn't have the luxury of allowing myself to be vulnerable like he wanted me to. If I tapped into my deeper emotions, they'd drown me, and I didn't have anyone around who could help pull me out of the water.

At the end of our hour, he said he wanted to see me once a week, but I never went back. If he couldn't give me some sort of psychological tricks to use on Ray to make him go away, what use was he? Survival first. Feelings later.

It was a page from Leviticus this time.

If a priest's daughter defiles herself by becoming a prostitute, she disgraces her father; she must be burned in the fire.

I stood in our kitchen and laughed. "Since when is dad a priest?" The joke for Angela's benefit being that I wasn't contradicting the prostitute part.

Angela didn't laugh. A few days earlier, she and Mom had driven up to the house and found a surprise. In the past, a surprise would be something like a plastic grocery bag full of vegetables out of some church member's garden hanging off our doorknob. This time it was a wide-open front door. She parked the van, ran up the front steps, and yanked the door shut so animals couldn't wander in, but there was no way she was she going in there until Dad got home.

It was possible Angela or Mom hadn't shut the door all the way when they left that morning. It was just as possible that Ray had been in the house again.

It wasn't so much the breaks-ins that made us nervous (though, they did). It was the never knowing. Every morning, people wake up and have a pretty good idea about what's going to happen to them that day. Eat breakfast. Go to school or work. Come home. Eat dinner. Go to bed. There's a lot of comfort in knowing what comes next. We didn't have that comfort anymore.

Travis heard back from the lab. They didn't find any fingerprints on the Sprite can. Dad's webcam had filmed Ray driving up and down our road at strange times during the day, but Ray told one of our elders, Mike, that a coworker had borrowed his truck. Besides, the police said driving down our road wasn't a crime.

We still didn't have any solid evidence. All we had were Ray's odd behaviors around me, his history of mental illness, and his history with his ex-wife. It wasn't enough to arrest him. It wasn't enough to keep us safe.

Not long after the Leviticus Bible page showed up, a state trooper decided to ask Ray some questions. Maybe if he put some pressure on him, Ray would crack and fess up.

Mom and Travis told me all about it later, but the only question I remember was, "Why did we find your fingerprints in Kristy's closet?" and that one sticks out because nobody ever *did* find any fingerprints in my closet. I don't know how ethical it was for that trooper to lie to Ray, but maybe when the law prevents you from arresting someone who's clearly guilty and dangerous, you get frustrated.

"And do you know what he said?" Mom asked, without giving me a chance at guessing. "Because he helped us move you into your dorm room."

Which was obviously a lie. If an innocent person was asked about their fingerprints showing up somewhere they couldn't possibly have been, they'd say, "I have no idea how my fingerprints could've gotten there since *I was never there*."

Ray couldn't say that because he knew he *had* been in my room, and for all he knew, he left some fingerprints. But that *still* wasn't evidence. *We* knew he was lying. *Travis* knew he was lying. The *state trooper* knew he was lying. He even told Dad that Ray was definitely the one doing all these things. Ray couldn't keep his stories straight, and the trooper had seen enough people lie to recognize it. But, as far as the other police officers and our church council members knew, maybe Ray *had* helped me move into my dorm room, and then my family got mad at him for some reason and we all agreed to lie and say he was stalking me.

It didn't matter what Ray did, or how obvious it was that he was doing it. We weren't going to get any resolution from the police, even though we had some police officers on our side. It's almost impossible to get a stalker arrested under anti-stalking laws. Even police officers who believe victims and understand the danger usually can't help. My family did everything we could to work through the system, but we were just spinning our wheels.

CHAPTER FIFTEEN

When I was seventeen, I did something stupid. Well, I did a lot of stupid things, but one thing really stands out.

It was 1998, and our youth group leader decided we all needed to kiss dating good-bye. She started pushing something called courtship. It was what good, young Christians did instead of dating.

Boy meets girl. Boy likes girl. Boy asks girl's father for permission to court her, with the intention of eventually marrying her. Boy and girl go on chaperoned outings until they officially get engaged.

I didn't think that sounded like a very good way of getting to know a person. What teenager is completely open and honest when a chaperone is hanging around? How would a girl ever really know who she was marrying? Of course, the point wasn't to get to know one another. The whole point was to keep the couple pure. You can't have sex if you're never left alone.

Our church leaders had a lot to say about purity. For a girl, her virginity was the greatest gift she could give to her future husband. To protect that gift, girls had to dress modestly so we wouldn't tempt the boys around us and cause them to sin. Like Paul wrote in Romans, "Make up your mind not to put any stumbling block or obstacle in the way of a brother or sister."

We weren't girls. We weren't sisters in Christ. We were objects of temptation and dangerous to the men around us.

How far apart can "object of temptation" and "object of obsession" really be?

Of course, when Paul talked about stumbling blocks he was making a point about Jewish dietary laws, not short skirts, but we only talked about short skirts and the hazards of being within three feet of the opposite sex. Because it was easier to tell the girls to cover up than to tell the boys and men to control their impulses and stop objectifying us.

We learned a first kiss should be saved for our wedding day (I'd already failed on that account) and hand-holding was a gateway drug to premarital sex. It wasn't enough to avoid physical intimacy. We also had to avoid emotional intimacy before marriage. One night, in front of the rest of the youth group, our leader told me that Ben could never give his whole heart to me because he'd already given it away to his ex-girlfriends just by dating them.

Shortly after that, a rumor started up that Angela and Daniel were having sex. When our youth group leader caught wind of it, she didn't go to my sister and ask her about it. She didn't tell the other kids to stop gossiping. She believed the lie.

She'd seen Daniel's car sitting in the church parking lot before youth group one night, and the windows were all fogged up. If she'd bothered to tap on the window, she'd have found out the windows were fogged up because Angela and Daniel had just come back from Sonic on a cool night and had a bunch of hot fast food in there with them. How do I know that? Because I was in the back seat pestering them to, "Come on! Just give me a *few* fries."

Angela and Daniel quit coming to youth group after that. Then more kids started dropping out. I'd put so much effort into building our youth group, and it was all coming apart. But I was a kid and she was an adult, so what could I do about it? I didn't have any control over who our youth group leader was. That was an elected position. And I didn't have any control over what the youth group leader taught us. All I could do was blow off some steam by creating a satirical website about her courtship classes.

Three of us sat in my kitchen one evening, after another night of courtship class, and came up with goofy top-ten countdowns and "You Know You're Gonna Have Sex If . . . " lists. We sent the link to one other person, who we knew would appreciate the humor, and then forgot all about it.

Several months later, Dad walked into the house and told me our courtship pushing youth group leader (who was no longer our leader by then and wasn't even attending our church anymore) had seen the website, and now I had to go to a church council meeting because I was the only person it could be traced back to since it was hosted on my family's GeoCities site.

At barely eighteen, I sat around a small table with Elmer, Dad, and our all-male elders to discuss top-ten sex lists and explain how the Internet worked. No, putting up a website was not the same thing as putting up a billboard in town. No, people from town wouldn't just happen across that website. You had to know the exact address, or you couldn't get to it.

A girl who had some minor teenage beef with me had showed it to my youth group leaders. She didn't accidentally stumble upon it, and nobody else who knew them was going to accidentally find it. Besides, some of the things on that website were word-for-word quotes straight from my youth group leader's mouth.

The elders wanted to know why I was mad enough to do it, and I told them I didn't like how she treated me like a sinner for having a boyfriend. What she'd said to me about Ben was mean-spirited and hurtful. That was about the time I started crying, and all the middle-aged men at the table got even more uncomfortable than they already were.

Still, they thought it was in bad taste and wanted me to apologize. I refused. I figured the website was more like a diary page than anything else. It was meant to be private, and I hadn't intentionally hurt anyone with it. Why should I apologize when our youth leader didn't have to apologize for teaching us all that courtship garbage or believing a rumor about my sister?

I should have just apologized, though. If I had cooperated, it might have made things easier on me a few months later when I was the subject of another church council meeting.

Ray got spooked after the state trooper questioned him, which might have made him to back off, if it weren't for our church council. Because I wasn't at the meeting, I had to rely on what I was told by people who were there. To be fair, the people who relayed the information to me were on my side, and they were worked up while telling me about it, but knowing all the people involved as well as I did, I painted a decent picture of it in my head.

Dad sat in the front pew and glanced from Ray to Jackie. He said he thought they'd previously decided non-council members couldn't attend meetings if they weren't on the agenda.

Jackie pretended it wasn't true, though her husband, Scott, said he thought it *was* true, but she couldn't find those minutes, so she suggested they just hear what Ray had to say. What could it hurt?

Mom and Travis sat together, right behind Dad, and stared Ray down as he sat across the church, next to Jackie, and said he didn't want secular authorities to judge him. He wanted to be judged by the church.

Mom smacked a hand down on top of Dad's pew and said Ray lied to the state trooper about his fingerprints being in my closet, and Dad and Travis backed her up. He never helped move me out. You'd think that'd be enough to convince the others in the room that Ray was a big liar, because both of my parents were sitting there saying it was a lie, and a police officer was sitting there saying it was a lie, but you'd be wrong.

One elder, Paul, sat quietly because he knew the whole situation was wrong, and he liked me, and he liked Dad, but he'd known Elmer for forever, and he'd never make a move against a friend. Ben, who shouldn't even have been there since he was no longer on the church council, sat in the last pew with his shoulders hunched and head bowed to the floor, hoping nobody would ask him to speak because he didn't even want to be there, but his family made him come.

Another elder, Mike, chimed in with some follow-up questions. He didn't want to believe anyone was a liar, even though someone there *had* to be. Ray started in again about how my family was persecuting him and how evil secular authority was. Travis, the only representative of that secular authority in the room, got fed up and shouted him down with his booming voice.

Dad tried to calm everyone down, but Mom was done. She stood up and revoked her church membership. Travis stood up right behind her and did the same before they marched out together.

Since Dad was the pastor, it wasn't as easy for him to get dramatic, so he said he wasn't sure he could continue preaching on Sunday if Ray was sitting in church. He asked to take some time off to sort things out. It was a reasonable request, and Paul and Mike probably would've been fine with it, but Elmer told Dad we weren't allowed to stay in the parsonage if Dad didn't preach. He was paid to preach, after all, and the rent-free parsonage, our home, was part of that payment.

Hearing about that meeting wounded parts of me I

didn't know could be hurt. They were willing to hear Ray out, but not me. I wasn't even invited to the meeting. Or to *any* meeting. They wanted to make sure Ray could continue to worship with his church on Sunday, but they didn't care that I couldn't.

Travis was the only non-blood relative who stood up for me, and he hadn't known me nearly as long as the rest of them had. I'd come into that church at fourteen. I'd helped with Vacation Bible School and pancake breakfasts and building projects. I cleaned the church every week for years, scrubbing toilets and pulling all sorts of disgusting things out of the hymnal slots. But that didn't matter. It didn't matter that I'd brought in my friends to grow the church and Ray hadn't brought in anyone. If you factored in the wife and sons who left him, he was actually in the negatives compared to me.

I'll never understand why the same elders who asked me to apologize about a joke website wouldn't ask a grown man to attend a different church for a few months until all this got sorted out. I'll never understand why people who had known my family for years would think we'd go around making up lies about someone who had eaten our food and slept on our couch.

I'll never understand how Ben could say he loved me and then sit there and say nothing at all. They say actions speak louder than words, but sometimes inaction speaks loudest of all. I'd wanted him to make a choice, and his silence showed he had.

CHAPTER SIXTEEN

My hair was pulled up into a tight, scalp-numbing ponytail. *Seventeen* magazine told me a girl appears more confident with her hair up and out of her face, and I could sure use the illusion of confidence. A pile of pictures, notes, and whatever random relationship totems I could find sat on my bedroom desk, my engagement ring sparkling on top of the stack.

It'd taken some waffling and an emergency visit from one of my best friends, Louise, which involved renting a hotel room so we could stay up all night and talk while I chain-smoked menthol cigarettes, but I had made my decision. After that church council meeting, what else could I do? I loved Ben, but love wasn't enough. I couldn't be with someone who wouldn't stick up for me. Louise said I deserved better, and even though I wasn't sure better existed anywhere out there, I had to give it a shot.

Work boots thumped down the hall, and I glanced in the mirror one last time to check for hair bumps. Ben walked into my bedroom and started with, "Hey—" but stopped when I turned to him without my usual smile. His eyes moved down to the desk, and he slumped against the doorframe, waiting for me to tear into him.

I pointed to the bed, and he sat, back arched forward, head turned down. He must have looked the same way at the church council meeting, and that thought got my anger up again. "This—" I paused as he made eye contact and fizzled out a little of my indignant spark. That miserable expression etched itself into my brain. Wet eyes. Heavy brows. And a definite look of resignation. Like this was inevitable, no matter what either of us wanted.

"This isn't working," I tried again.

He didn't say anything, and I wondered whether he understood what I meant, or if he was doing that silent thing he so often did. To clear up any confusion, I said, "We have to break up."

His face caved in, and tears splashed onto his coveralls. I hadn't expected that. I didn't think he'd jump for joy or anything. I mean, nobody likes getting dumped. But I didn't think it'd take him by surprise either. Things had been rough between us since the first break-in. We'd barely spoken since I left for UCA, and when we did, we tended to fight about Ray. And how could he expect me not to react to that church council meeting? But there he was, crying on my bed like I'd ripped out his heart. Maybe I shouldn't have stacked all those pictures up for him to see when he walked in.

He choked out a one-word reply. "Why?"

I recited his transgressions with as little emotion as possible to counterbalance his tears. He didn't believe Ray was stalking me. Or, if he did believe it, he wouldn't admit it and stand up to his family. He hadn't defended me at the council meeting. I'd barely seen or heard from him over the past month, even though he knew I was struggling to cope.

In reply, he stayed silent about my own failings. He didn't shake a finger at me for coming home high. He didn't express his frustration about how ripped up magazine and Bible pages had monopolized the time we spent together. He didn't berate me for not just coming right out and asking him to come see me in Conway instead of expecting him to know I wanted him to.

I couldn't see him anymore, that boy who'd apologized for kissing me. Who'd climbed into my twin bed when I was sick and held me. Who'd organized tool chests and measured wrapping paper and welded Valentine's cards out of metal. And maybe he couldn't see me anymore either. How could he reach me through all the new edges I'd grown?

He told me once I wasn't like other people. "It's like everyone else is driving down the road, and they're watching out for the next bend that's up aways so they can turn the wheel in time and won't go off the road. But you're not like that. You're not looking right in front of the car like everyone else. You're staring way out there, miles away, at the mountains in the distance, and planning what you'll do when you hit those."

I was always more aware of the future than the present. I'd plan and hope and drive myself forward, even if I ran off the road a little sometimes because I wasn't paying much attention to what was right in front of me. And that might have worked out. Ben watched out for what was right in front of us, and I watched out for what was coming way down the road. Except we'd stopped doing that. Ben had shifted his focus to the future. This Ray situation was just temporary, and it'd work out eventually, so he chose to ignore the present and focus on what came after. But all I could see was now. Ray was a problem *right now* that needed to be dealt with. I'd never get to the mountains if I couldn't detour around him. Ray controlled what came next for me, and all I could control was how I reacted in the moment to every new, twisted move he made. Now was all that mattered because now was all there was.

There was no way to win here. I knew it. Ben knew it. If he stood by me, he stood against his father and sister. He'd have me, but lose them. I was backed into a more dangerous corner. Even if I lied and said Mom made it all up and she'd been behind the whole thing, and Ben's family embraced me as one of their own, I still couldn't win. Ray would still be there—a threat no matter which side I chose. No matter what choice I'd make, I'd lose.

Ben had one defensive move to counter me with. "But I love you."

His face blurred. I hadn't stomped my emotions down as much as I'd thought. We cried together for a little while before I took a deep breath and shifted my gaze over to the corner. With all the fight drained out of my voice, I whispered, "I know you love me."

I wiped tears off my cheeks and turned back to him. He looked almost hopeful, and that's what stung the most. One way or another, I had to hurt him. If I stayed and tried to fight to keep our relationship together, his family would pull him apart. If I left, I'd be the one pulling him apart. At least this way he'd only lose me, and how big of a loss could that be if he couldn't even bring himself to speak up for me? He'd be grateful for it, in the end. He'd find another girl and tell her all about the horrible ex who broke his heart. Maybe that new girl would even write him a poem in pink gel ink.

I took a deep breath and laid it out as gently as I could. "You don't love me the way I need to be loved, and I can't be with you anymore."

My favorite character was Jane Eyre. She said she wasn't a bird and wouldn't be caged, but right then I wanted to be a bird more than anything. I wanted him to beg me. Cage me. Keep me. If he'd made any promise to do better, to be better, I'd have caved.

Ben tilted his head back down to stare at the floor and shed a few more silent tears, but he didn't make any promises. He nodded his head once, stepped over to my desk, placed the diamond ring in his shirt pocket, picked up the stack of pictures, and walked away.

CHAPTER SEVENTEEN

I'd like to say breaking up with Ben was a turning point for me. I blossomed into a full-fledged feminist heroine and realized I didn't need some man to make me happy. I took control of my life and never looked back.

In reality, two days later, I sat on my couch and stared at the phone across the room, thinking about the time Ben showed up at my house to surprise me with Pepsi and candy while I was studying for finals and how he always drove me anywhere I wanted to go because I didn't like to drive and he told me, "That's what boyfriends do."

He was proud when I got my scholarship, and he never raised his voice to me, and he laughed at my jokes . . . and I'd made a horrible mistake.

Maybe it wasn't too late. I could take it back, and we could find a way to work things out. Maybe we could even get married sooner than we'd talked about. If we were married, and I was officially part of his family, they'd *have* to look out for me.

What if I'd dumped the only person who'd ever want me? I broke up with Ben because he wouldn't defend me to his family, but what if *nobody* out there thought I was worth the amount of effort it'd take to say, "Hey, shut up," to one of their relatives? It was nice to hear I deserved better, but what if better wasn't out there?

Angela strolled through right as I decided to make the call. She paused when she noticed I was sitting around, staring intently at nothing at all. "What's up with you?"

I leapt up, all resolute. "I'm calling him."

"What? Ben?" She moved to block me, but I sidestepped her and kept heading for the phone. "That's the stupidest thing I've ever heard."

I whirled around on her. "Loving someone isn't stupid."

She crossed her arms and stared me down. "It is this time."

There were plenty of times I got annoyed enough with my little sister to haul off and whack her upside the head, but I never actually hated her. Right then, though, I got close. She didn't get it. She had Daniel, but who did I have? I was locked up in my dorm room, with no boyfriend, no family, no church. I had some kids to hang out with, but nobody who really loved me. Was it such a terrible thing to want to be loved? To want a little affection?

But I knew that even if I called Ben, even if he took me back, it wouldn't make any difference. I still wouldn't really have him in any way that mattered.

I moved away from the phone and started to cry, like I always do when I'm too frustrated for words. I'd always thought that all you had to do in life was figure out what the right thing to do was, and then do that thing. Simple as that. But there weren't any right choices here. All I could do was choose one crappy path or the other crappy path, and I had no idea which path actually had more crap to wade through.

Angela's scowl evaporated as I swiped tears off my face and sank back down onto the couch. My head dropped down into my hands. "I have no idea what I'm doing," I admitted into my palms.

She sat down beside me. "I don't think *any* of us knows what we're doing right now."

Matt walked into Erin's kitchen, draped an arm around my shoulders, and flooded me with that flirtatious smile he always used on girls. "Hey!" he said.

A couple of hours after Daniel dropped me back off at my dorm, Olivia and Luke (from Pine Creek's Class of 1999) showed up to see if I'd go over to Erin's with them since a group of kids we knew from Pine Creek were there. Staying at the dorm on my own with a tornado of "you will die alone" whizzing through my head didn't sound like it'd be as much fun, so I jumped at the chance to get out.

"So, what's new with you, anyway?" Nessa asked.

She rolled a pair of dice and then rolled her eyes when her new boyfriend laughed because she hadn't won whatever game they were playing. I sat on a bar stool, took another sip of the Zima I'd begged off her, and told her I'd broken up with Ben.

"Seriously?" Matt asked.

"Yep. I've been super single for three whole days." I picked up the dice and gave them a roll, even though I didn't understand the game.

I don't know if my roll was good or not because I fell backward off the stool. Except I hadn't fallen. Matt had grabbed hold of me, tipped me back into his arms, and kissed me.

And I let him.

I'd known him for a couple of years. He was cute and nice and in my yearbook, he'd written, "You looked really great at prom."

He set me back upright, and Nessa's face came into view again. Her eyes locked onto mine. "God, Matt," she said, "moving pretty fast there, aren't you?"

Nessa and I'd met in tenth grade. I was her straight-laced friend. The one who didn't drink or smoke pot or mess with boys.

I smiled at her. "It's OK."

She shrugged and grabbed the dice.

When I finished my Zima, Nessa handed me another one, and I finished that one too. I'd never had alcohol before. Once, when I was sixteen, a bunch of us girls had spent the night in a barn. Someone had smuggled a bottle of peach schnapps out there, and the other girls passed it around, but I just said no. Drinking was wrong, and I wasn't going to tell the other girls their business, but I could still set a good example and turn it down.

But I didn't turn things down anymore, and everyone

around me was generous with what they had. And they didn't judge me for drinking or smoking pot. Nobody here cared what I did. It was the only freedom I had anymore.

At some point, the apartment emptied out, and Matt and I sat on the couch, alone. And he kissed me again. And then our clothes were on the floor. And he held my hand and led me into the bathroom.

Ben didn't want me. My church didn't want me. At least they didn't want me as much as they wanted Ray. My family loved me, but they didn't want me around. Matt only wanted me for a little while, but it was something. I figured it didn't matter much, anyway. I wasn't a virgin anymore, and according to last year's youth group leader, that was what really mattered. Once it was gone, it was gone.

He said he wanted to "do it" in the shower. We laughed together and wiped water out of our eyes when we slipped and fell.

After he finished, I turned the shower off. Voices the falling water had masked rose and fell outside the bathroom door. The shower and the physical exertion had sobered us both up enough to realize we were stuck in the bathroom while our clothes were stuck in the living room, which was now full of our old schoolmates.

We stepped out of the tub, and I stared at him for a minute, waiting for him to take charge and fix the situation, since he was the guy and the whole thing was his idea in the first place. He didn't make a move, though, and he even seemed a little embarrassed. I rolled

Act Normal

my eyes at him, then cracked the bathroom door open. "Hey! Someone grab the clothes by the couch and toss them in."

There was an uproar from the living room. "Who's fucking in the bathroom?" one of the boys shouted back.

"Who are you in there with?" Nessa, who must have recognized my voice, shouted right behind him.

"Like, five guys. Who cares who I'm in here with? I need my clothes."

A girl's arm pushed the door open a little wider and thrust an armful of clothes at me. We pulled our pants on over our still dripping bodies and rejoined everyone in the living room, where we caught a little comment here and there, but it was late, and everyone was winding down, so we didn't suffer much.

Most people wandered out of the apartment or into one of the bedrooms. I sat on the couch, and Matt surprised me when he lay down with his head in my lap, started snoring, and trapped me there.

"Why'd you do that?"

I turned my head to the bar where Luke sat, a little unsteady on a barstool, brown hair flopping down into his face. "Why'd you have sex with *him*?"

Luke and I weren't exactly good friends, but you can't graduate high school with a class of about forty students and not have a pretty good feel for most people.

"Because he was there," I said. It was the truth.

Matt snored louder and shifted a little, but Luke ignored him. "I've been in love with you since ninth grade," he said, like Matt and I had ignored the rules of dibs.

I thought he was screwing with me. "Well, you never said anything." I swept a hand through the air over my chest and said, "And it's first come, first served around here."

He didn't laugh at the joke. Instead, he slipped off the bar stool and walked out. I felt bad then because maybe he hadn't been joking. He might have thought, since I was single now, he had a shot. Maybe he really did think he was in love with me, even if he didn't know me well enough for that to be true. Anyone who *did* know me well enough apparently *didn't* love me, even when they said they did.

That's what I liked about Matt. He didn't lie to me. He didn't think he was in love with me. He just wanted sex, and there was something reassuring about knowing exactly where I stood with someone. No guessing games or any actual vulnerability. In some twist-turn-y way, a one-night stand could make me feel grounded and in control.

I'd planned to marry the first boy I ever kissed. It wasn't hard to justify having sex with Ben. We loved each other, and I was pretty sure marriage vows could be applied retroactively. But drunk, impulsive bathroom sex with Matt was something completely different. There was no easy justification for that. I'd crossed a line with Ben, with my church, and with God. And I didn't care. Not one bit.

The next morning, Matt and I went for a sober round in one of the bedrooms that had a mattress on the floor.

After, I fell asleep there on the floor without bothering to get dressed first. Matt apparently left the room because I woke up when the door swung open, a cool draft hit me, and an unfamiliar boy's voice yelled, "There's a naked chick in here!"

I didn't open my eyes to see who was at the door. I didn't care. It was probably one of the boys from a couple of apartments over, but I wouldn't have cared much if the entire neighborhood had walked in. I hadn't had any privacy since Ray snatched my underwear back in August, so what difference did this make?

Footsteps stomped down the hall, and the door slammed shut. "Get out of there," another boy said to the overly excited neighbor.

"Just let her sleep," a girl said.

I stayed right where I was and drifted back into sleep. I was safe there, lying naked on the floor in an apartment full of boys, guarded by half-high teenagers I barely knew from high school. Home was dangerous. Church was dangerous. *This* was sanctuary.

CHAPTER EIGHTEEN

I'm not good with names. Maybe his name was Eddy. Or Jerry. Or Mike. There aren't all that many boy names floating around out there, so you'd think I would have remembered his name at some point, but it never did stick in my head.

The first time I met him, I heard a knock on Erin's door and opened it to find a big, red T-shirt in my face. I'm not short, so someone towering a full head above me is something I notice.

The next time he came over, he remembered me, but I didn't remember anything about him except that red shirt, so I said, "Hey, you're the shirt guy!" and after that, I always called him Shirt Guy, even though he'd frown and tell me, "My name's—" before my memory skipped like a crappy CD player and I'd land right back at Shirt Guy because I suck at giving nicknames almost as much as I suck at remembering names.

I'd been sitting on Cody and Luke's couch, next to the goateed Shirt Guy, for a few hours. I think. How long does it take to smoke a blunt with a handful of people and then stare at an unplugged Nintendo while imagining a game of Tetris? Three hours?

That was the day Shirt Guy flipped the blunt

Act Normal

backward in his mouth, winked, and gestured me over to him. I sat beside him, eyebrows up, trying to figure out what he wanted as his eyes started watering and he flapped his hands at me. Olivia saved us both by rushing over, sealing her lips over his, and inhaling the smoke from his mouth.

"It's called a shotgun," she explained to me.

"I didn't know. I've never done that before."

He nodded, eyes still glossy. "Burned my fucking tongue."

I laughed. "Why didn't you just take it back out?"

He turned red and coughed before recovering enough to ask, "Wanna get some food?"

I *always* want to get some food, so I climbed into his two-door and off we went through Conway. The sun was too bright, and I squinted out the windshield as he drove me around and pointed out a few places that probably would have been interesting, if I could have focused on them.

He pulled up alongside the police station and reached for the door handle. I sure focused on *that*. "Got to check in with my parole officer. I'll be right back."

If all my reflexes hadn't been on a delay timer, I'd have reached over and yanked his hand off the handle and asked him what the heck he was thinking, dragging my high-as-a-kite butt along on a ride to see his parole officer. But he was already out of the car and halfway down the sidewalk before that reaction kicked in.

Just what I needed. Shirt Guy was walking straight into the police station, blurry-eyed and mellow as all get-out. There was no way a police officer wouldn't realize he was high. They'd arrest him, and then he'd tell them he had a friend out in the car, waiting for him, and they'd come out to see me, and they'd know I was high too, and I'd get arrested, and Dad would have to come bail me out, and even though I was legally an adult, somehow my parents would find a way of keeping me even more locked up than they already did.

I could abandon him—just walk away—but I didn't know my way around Conway. I couldn't even get to the apartments if Olivia wasn't with me. I didn't own a cell phone, and even if I did, or if I used a pay phone, who could I call? I didn't have Luke's number, so Olivia wasn't an option. Angela and Daniel were in school. The only other number I had memorized was Ben's, and that wasn't going to work. "Oh, hey. It's me. The girl who just broke up with you. I'm high and cruising around with some guy who's also high, even though I don't know his name, and well, it's so silly, but I'm about to get arrested. Come pick me up, 'kay?"

About the time I started to seriously consider hitchhiking back to campus, Shirt Guy came strolling out the glass doors without any police officers jerking on his cuffed hands from behind. He slid back into the driver's seat and off we went. "Pot isn't like alcohol," he said, even though I hadn't mentioned either. "Alcohol makes you a bad driver, but pot makes you a better driver. You're a lot more cautious when you smoke pot."

We cautiously drove through a few more intersections and pulled into the parking lot of a strip mall. "I gotta pick something up," he said.

He held the glass door of the tattoo shop open for me, which struck me as odd. The only two boys who'd shown me this level of courtesy were Nick, the smart, clean-cut, button-down boy who'd had a crush on me a couple years back and what's-his-name, the pot-smoking, gauge-wearing, parole-officer-having boy who'd tried to get me to shotgun him.

I wondered what Nick was doing. Probably not visiting a tattoo shop.

"Got any tattoos?" Shirt Guy asked from somewhere above my head.

I looked around at all the tattoo designs taped to the walls. Looney Tunes characters. Barbed wire. Howling wolves. Celtic knots. Women with strap-on cartoon breasts. "No, but I've wanted one for a while."

His eyes lit up. "Get one now," he suggested.

"I don't know what to pick."

He gestured toward the walls. "Look around. Get one that means something to you."

He walked over to the counter to get his new gauges, and I wandered around the small shop, trying to pick a design that meant something to me. I knew what I would've picked a year ago. I'd sketched it out on notebook paper when I should have been paying attention in Spanish. A small, simple cross with an ichthys running around it. I'd wanted to get it tattooed on my ankle when I turned eighteen because it meant something to me. *This is who I am.*

A wall of religious tattoos stared me down. A hand

with a nail through it. A cross with a crown of thorns hanging off the top. A heart on fire.

Was I still Christian enough to get a cross tattooed on my ankle? I still believed in Jesus, but belief wasn't enough. Like the Bible says, even the demons believe. It takes faith—real faith—to be a Christian. And I hadn't even prayed since before Ben and I broke up. It seemed pointless to pray to God when he obviously wasn't listening.

No. I couldn't get a cross. A tattoo shouldn't be a lie.

My empty stomach tightened along with my jaw. What was I doing here? Maybe I couldn't get my cross and fish, because that wasn't who I was anymore, but was *this* who I was? Really? Was I someone who risked getting arrested for a hamburger? Someone who left a safe and crowded apartment with a stranger twice my size? Didn't I used to be smart? Didn't I used to care about consequences?

"Pick something yet?" He was beside me again, holding a small brown paper bag.

"Can't find anything."

How can you permanently mark yourself with an identity when you don't have one anymore?

He held the door for me again and placed a large hand on my back to guide me outside, into the too-bright day. We never did eat.

CHAPTER NINETEEN

My friends, Alex and Louise, brought Jeff up with them from Little Rock just to "hang out," but I figured it was their way of nudging me farther away from Ben and farther away from screwing my way through our high school yearbook. The week before, I'd shown them the mean bruise on my lower back from "doing Matt in the shower."

The four of us ate at Burger King and then cruised around Conway listening to music while Alex used his radio announcer's voice to make obscene jokes. Even with my stupid comments (that Jeff didn't think were funny) and almost as stupid sit-dancing in the back seat, I had fun.

On any other weekend, I'd have tried to convince my parents to let me come home, but since I'd broken up with Ben, I didn't see much point in heading back to Pine Creek anytime soon.

As I walked up the stairs to my hall, I decided to call Louise the next day and ask her to explain me to Jeff. She could tell him I never made a good first impression, but I was fine if you ignored all the dumb crap I said. I wasn't interested in dating Jeff—or anyone—but he seemed like a decent person to hang out with. I thought maybe we could all get together again the next weekend.

Mom and Dad had lent me the family station wagon on my last trip home, so I was more mobile than I had been before. I'd spent more time at Borders over the last couple of weeks than at the apartments. I'd even started going to my classes again and was trying to catch up on all the reading I'd ignored. If I could pull my grades up to a C for the semester, I'd have to work my tail off during the winter semester to boost my GPA, but I could keep my scholarship. It was totally doable.

This turnaround in my attitude was mostly due to how quiet things had gotten at home. Not a single thing happened after the church council meeting. No phone calls. No Bible pages. No magazine brides. Nothing.

Maybe the state trooper's questions had scared Ray away. Maybe he was satisfied since Ben and I weren't together anymore. It didn't really matter. It was just nice to feel like I could breathe.

I still checked the closets every time I walked into my dorm room, but I was starting to feel a little ridiculous about being so paranoid, like I'd made too big of a deal about it.

When I walked into my dorm room that night, several message notifications were flashing on the answering machine. They were all from Mom, asking me to call her back.

Angela answered on the first ring. "Where were you?"

I was so surprised by her accusatory tone, it didn't even occur to me to be pissed off. "Out with Alex and

Louise. Why?"

She gave an impatient, snort-like noise of disapproval. "What's wrong with Alex and Louise? God, Angela. Mom wanted me to call. Is she up?"

She handed the phone off to Mom, and the first words out of her mouth were, "Stay calm," which always means I'm about to hear something that'll make me definitely not calm, followed by, "We're all fine."

A million different nightmare scenarios ran through my head. Ray tried to kidnap Angela, and she had to fight him off. He stole Dad's van, packed it full of illegal guns, and turned Dad into the police. Maybe he'd grabbed a gun, stood on our front lawn, and stuffed the barrel into his mouth.

She said there had been a fire in my bedroom the night before. Ray had waited until the middle of the night, pulled the screen off my bedroom window, broken through the outdated lock, and climbed in.

First, he spent some time indulging in his favorite hobby of going through my private things. He took a T-shirt out of my closet and spread it out on my bed, right where I would have been lying if I'd been there. Next, he took a Barbie doll off the shelf above my desk. Mom had sewn her fluffy, white wedding dress when I was eight. He laid Bridal Barbie on top of my shirt, set her on fire, and climbed back out the window.

The screeching smoke detector woke my parents, and they ran out into the smoky hall. Dad smothered the flames before they spread past my bed.

"Is my pillow ruined?" was all I could think to ask,

because what else can you say to that?

I couldn't really process what I was hearing, not emotionally, at least. It was like listening to an urban legend that Mom swore her friend's aunt's ex-husband had really been there to witness. I heard what she told me, and I took it all in, but felt numb and removed from the whole ordeal. It hadn't *really* happened in my house. It hadn't *really* been my bed. It couldn't have been.

Logically, I could understand why Angela was so irate. She'd gotten way too close to dying in a house fire last night. She was home dealing with the fallout while I was out having a good time.

Mom said they saved the bed, but my pillow, comforter, shirt, and doll were ruined. "Which shirt?"

The white one, with blue flowers embroidered around the bottom. My favorite one. My emotional cogs finally started grinding again. I'd almost brought that shirt back to Conway with me last time I was home, but I'd forgotten to grab it. Some completely irrational part of my brain said it was my fault. If I'd brought the shirt with me, he wouldn't have set the fire. If I could just get my act together and do all the right things, this would end.

My parents called the police, but since they hadn't actually seen Ray in the house, the police wouldn't arrest him. As far as they knew, maybe my parents had set the fire on purpose so they could blame it on Ray. They were skeptical that a man could climb through a window and rummage around in a bedroom without waking anyone up. Three years later, another long-haired, bearded man would climb through a window and abduct a fourteen-year-old girl from her home in Utah. Until she's rescued, people will be skeptical that a man could have climbed through her home's window without waking her parents too.

I wanted to hop in the station wagon and drive straight home, but Mom told me to stay put. I was safe in the dorm. "But *you're* not safe," I said. That Bible verse about a priest's daughter and fire shot through my head. Now I understood why Travis had taken it so seriously.

Mom thought I was in a lot more danger than they were, even when I pointed out that all Ray had to do was douse the parsonage in gas and light the whole thing up. A smoke detector wouldn't do much good against that.

We hung up, and I spent the rest of the night lying awake on the bottom bunk wondering if the police would make me identify the remains of my charred family.

Would I get a phone call or would a police officer drive to Conway to tell me they were all dead? No, they wouldn't call. Travis would feel like he owed it to me to come out in person. He'd drive over, pull me out of class one morning, and tell me to "stay calm" just like Mom had, and then he'd drive me back to Pine Creek. We'd pull up to the blackened parsonage, and the roof would be caved in over Angela's bedroom. I'd find scorch marks running up the walls of what used to be the living room. Travis would say they were asleep and it was the smoke that killed them, not the flames, and they probably didn't feel anything. But then I'd walk through the rubble and find three sets of fingernail marks on the front door because they'd tried to get out, but Ray wouldn't let them out, and I wasn't there to help.

Ray would come to their funeral. Just to gloat. Just to prove he could do anything he wanted—take anything he wanted—and nobody would do anything about it. And then I'd really be all on my own because Ben was gone, and my church family was gone, and my parents were gone, and even my little sister was gone, and I couldn't do anything to stop him.

The next day, my attention was split between the psychology textbook in my lap and Christina Aguilera's new music video on Cody and Luke's TV. Cody pointed the remote at the screen and turned it up while my laundry tumbled dry in the kitchen. "She's just trying to be Britney," he said.

"Totally." I leaned my head on the armrest and tried to prop my book up one-handed.

I must have dozed off because I woke up to Luke yelling in from the kitchen. "Whose are these?"

He walked into the living room twirling a pair of black underwear around his index finger. I lifted my head up off the couch a little. "Mine."

He made some joke about my underwear being in his living room, but I ignored him and closed my eyes again. He sat down on the couch near my curled-up legs when I didn't take the bait. "What?" he asked.

Olivia paused her folding and answered for me. "Some more stuff happened at her house."

I'd mentioned my Ray problem before, usually when I was high and started talking just to hear myself talk, but I'd always played it off like it wasn't a big deal, or like it was some kind of joke. "Yeah, this old hippie's obsessed with me. How crazy is that?"

The boys wanted to know what happened, so I sat up and told them about the fire.

Luke tossed my underwear into Olivia's laundry basket, and Cody leaned forward in his chair. "Where does this guy live?"

I didn't know exactly. My parents had been out to his place, but I'd never gone. "Could you find out?" Luke asked.

"I could ask my mom."

Cody nodded and narrowed his eyes. "Find out and let us know. We'll take care of it."

Luke nodded along.

"What does 'take care of it' mean?" I asked.

Cody leaned back in his chair and splayed his legs out. "We could smash up his car. Slit his tires or something. Keep him from getting from his place to your place."

"It'd be a warning," Luke added.

Luke may not have known me well enough to love me, but he loved me well enough to defend me, which was more than I'd gotten from Ben or the members of our church council.

I wanted to tell them to go for it, but what would happen when Ray walked outside and saw a couple of teenage boys wailing on his truck? Did they think he'd stand there and watch? I assumed Ray had guns. He was into all that Y2K survivalist end-of-civilization-as-we-know-it stuff, and everyone knew those guys had stockpiles of guns and ammo. The boys had no idea how much danger they were offering to put themselves in.

But at least they'd offered. I'd been waiting for someone, anyone, to offer me any kind of practical help. That offer spoke volumes. They believed me right off the bat, without question, because they knew what kind of person I was. On top of their unreserved faith in my honesty, they were willing to stick their necks out for me. I was worth the risk because I was one of them. And that was all I'd ever really wanted. To belong somewhere. I felt so much affection for those two boys I'd barely spoken to all through high school that I couldn't possibly say yes and put them in any danger.

"I don't want y'all getting into trouble. We'll let the police handle it," I said, even though I knew damn well the police couldn't handle anything.

CHAPTER TWENTY

The closer I got to Pine Creek, the more kudzu climbed over telephone poles and trees. Ben had told me about it. Before we started dating, he took me for a ride on his four-wheeler. I sat behind him and held onto his waist as he drove through trees and down paths I couldn't see. When he pulled off for a little while, I asked what all that green stuff was.

"Kudzu," he'd said, an invasive species. During the Great Depression, farmers thought it was the solution to soil erosion. They planted it on purpose, but they didn't realize how quickly it spread or how hard it was to kill. It reached beyond farms and into the forest where it snaked up ancient trees, covered the canopy, and blocked out almost all sunlight from reaching the plants and trees below. People called kudzu the vine that ate the south, but that vine didn't eat the south. It starved it.

By the time I hit town, the sun was down. I drove straight home, but found an empty driveway and dark windows. I wasn't brave enough to walk into my house alone, especially after dark. There were too many rooms and closets to check. I turned around and headed to the first gas station in town to call Daniel. I told him I was in town, and he made me wait at the gas station for him so we could go back to the house together.

Fifteen minutes later, I stepped up onto my porch right behind him. He reached for the screen door handle and turned back to me before pulling it open. "Stay here. If I yell, run to your car."

I looked around at the dark trees and empty dirt road. Ray could just as easily be hiding in the trees. "No way. I'm too freaked out."

We walked in together. Daniel gave my room a quick check first, then moved on to my parents' room before I could do more than peek in at the new blue comforter on my bed. Side by side, we Scooby-Doo crept through each room, waiting for a monster to pop out of one of the closets. I don't know what we thought two unarmed teenagers could do if we found Ray. Luckily, all the closets were empty, so we didn't have to find out.

After our search, Daniel promised to stay until my parents got home, and settled onto the couch to watch TV while I circled back to my bedroom to survey the damage.

I thought it'd smell like smoke or I'd find singed walls, but other than the new comforter and a flatter pillow, there wasn't any evidence of the fire. My parents had already removed the burned comforter and Barbie Bride.

Scanning across my desk, I noticed someone had moved my lipstick. Inside the clear lid, the tapered end was smashed and flattened. Had Ray put my lipstick on? I'd have laughed if I wasn't so horrified by the thought of something that had touched my lips also touching his.

Act Normal

That's when I realized I'd missed something much more obvious than lipstick. The large mirror that hung over my desk was gone. I assumed Ray had taken it, but I couldn't figure out how he could have gotten the mirror out the window before the smoke alarm went off. Maybe he'd slid it out the window right before setting the fire.

I tossed my ruined lipstick into a desk drawer, so it'd at least be out of sight, and started toward my door so I could join Daniel. A flash of mint green behind the desk caught my eye. I crouched down to find my mirror sitting on the floor, wedged between the wall and desk.

At first I thought it'd fallen off the wall, but it was facing the wrong way, with the brown papered back facing the room. Someone had taken it off the wall and shoved it behind my desk on purpose. When I pulled it free and flipped it around, I saw why. Ray had used my blood red lipstick to draw an eye on the mirror that watched me sleep.

He was always watching.

What if I'd been home? I'd stayed on campus to hang out with Alex and Louise, but what if I hadn't? I was always driving home without permission, just like I had tonight. I could have been asleep in my bed when he climbed through the window. Had he come to burn *me* and settled for my doll?

That night, Angela and Daniel sat in my room and showed me the stack of Bible pages Ray left on my desk the night of the fire. I read the underlined passages.

Your daughter [he'd crossed out 'in-law'] is guilty of prostitution, and as a result she is now pregnant. Have her burned to death.

Angela pointed to the underlined words after that passage and read them aloud, "For you have made your sisters appear righteous." She looked up at me. "Well, thanks for that, I guess."

I was too worked up to make jokes. These were serious threats. "I don't understand what you're still doing here. If Dad wants to stick around and be a pastor, fine. But you and Mom need to go. How can you even sleep here?"

Her eyes narrowed. "You think I sleep?"

"Well, I don't sleep either," I shot back, like it was a competition.

She said Dad sent her and Mom to his friend's empty apartment over Radio Shack the night after the fire. He'd sat up, hoping to catch Ray if he came back, but nothing happened that night.

The next night, Daniel sat up all night in the dark church, watching out the window, but Ray stayed away that night too.

I didn't understand why things had been so quiet, then all of a sudden we were getting fires. "That was Mike," Angela said. Ray had been sleeping at his house for a while, and Mike kept taking his truck keys every night. He thought it'd prove Ray was innocent if we got messed with when he had an alibi. Mike wasn't happy when Dad told him nothing had happened the whole time Ray had been staying with him.

Mike was one of the elders who'd helped baptize me in a creek two years before. He'd held out his hand to

Act Normal

steady me so I wouldn't slip and fall as I took heavy steps up out of the running water and onto the gravel bank where the rest of our church waited to greet me as a new member.

Ray hadn't stayed with Mike's family the night of the fire. Of course, Mike didn't think that proved anything. A close family friend couldn't possibly be threatening the pastor's daughter.

Daniel and Angela had scoured the church property over the past couple of days, searching for evidence. They found some tire tracks out in the field behind the parsonage and a large rock under my bedroom window. Daniel figured Ray moved it there to stand on so he could climb in more easily. He and Angela took pictures of anything they thought might help the police pin it on Ray.

The whole situation was ridiculous. My family was being terrorized. The police couldn't, or wouldn't, do anything to stop it. My case was being investigated by two seventeen-year-olds, and my church council refused to believe the man we all knew suffered from delusions just might be the person who was doing all these things.

Instead of our church leaders turning on Ray for going after their pastor's teenage daughter, they'd turned on Mom. Jackie had started telling people she thought Mom was possessed and her demon was framing poor Ray. And the theory that was even crazier than demonic possession was that Mom hated Ray and was framing him on her own. Why? Well, nobody could answer that one. Just like nobody could explain why all of Ray's favorite Old Testament scriptures were showing up at my house on ripped out Bible pages. Mom wasn't all that familiar with the Old Testament. Even if she had gone off the deep end and was suffering some mental breakdown, she wouldn't magically be fluent in obscure Old Testament scriptures about burning whores.

Neither of Jackie's theories made any sense, even if you ignored the outlandish demon aspect. Because there was one thing that would have really helped frame him, though it never happened. One of those movie-type cut-out letter messages could have shown up that said, "Dear Kristy, I'm totally going to murder you so hard. Love, your smelly hippie pal, Ray." Nothing came close to tying so directly to Ray. If Mom was framing him, she was seriously incompetent.

But as long as people were focused on her, they weren't focused on Ray. And as long as they weren't focused on Ray, he could keep on doing whatever he wanted, and it was looking more and more like what he wanted was a corpse.

CHAPTER TWENTY-ONE

The red numbers on my alarm clock told me I'd been waiting over three hours for him to climb through my bedroom window. I didn't want to think about what would have happened if I'd been home the night of the fire, but I couldn't shake the thought, especially since I was home and lying in the bed he'd torched.

I kept my back to the window and cocooned myself in the new comforter that still smelled like the plastic bag it came in. And I waited. My parents' snores traveled to me in waves, across the hallway, through their shut door and past my own. The house was quiet, other than that.

We had all checked the window lock before I went to bed, but they'd checked it the night of the fire too, and that hadn't done much good.

The new pillow was too flat for side sleeping, but I didn't want to roll onto my back. If I did that, I'd have to look at the window.

Mom and Dad didn't want me at home, but I was fed up with hiding and fed up with Ray going after them to get at me. I wanted to be done with it. I was tired of being afraid of every noise and every phone call and every long-haired head that passed me in the store. I couldn't live like this.

Maybe he'd notice the white station wagon in the parking lot, realize I'm home, and climb through my window again. Maybe he'd be satisfied with killing me and leave Mom, Dad, and Angela alone.

He'd leave behind enough evidence to get caught. I'd scratch at him and trap some skin under my fingernails. He'd pay then. They'd all pay. My ghost would stick around and haunt every last person on that church council.

But he probably wanted to punish my family for keeping me away. Maybe he'd finish with me before I could scream out a warning, light me on fire, and the whole house would go up in flames before they'd know what was happening. At least we'd go together. At least I wouldn't be left here all alone. And Angela's room was all the way at the other end of the house. She might get out in time, and she had Daniel, and his family would take care of her.

He hadn't come yet, though, and I was exhausted. I closed my eyes and drifted through half-awake nightmares where everything was too hot to touch, and I ran toward a police officer, but no matter how fast or how far I ran, he slid away, always just on the horizon, and when I screamed at him, no sound came out.

A twig snapped, and my eyes shot open. Real life or dream? I couldn't tell, but my heart started pounding away. Was it a raccoon? A dog? Ray? I held my breath and strained to hear through the rise and falls of those dual snores. I swear I heard something like leaves brushing up against a nylon jacket.

Glass and that joke of a lock separated us.

I was going to die. I was really, really going to die. And he'd make sure I suffered before I went because I didn't do what he wanted, and I knew I was supposed to be OK with that because heaven is a wonderful place, but I didn't want to find out, and it turned out I was all right with living in constant fear as long as I got to keep breathing and I didn't have to burn.

I don't want to burn.

My body started shaking, even though the room was warm. I started to cry and did my best to keep quiet and muffle down the sobs that wanted to break out.

Another muffled noise from outside. I definitely didn't dream that.

Before I could even think about it, I rolled off my bed and onto the floor. I peeked over the top of the bed at the window. There was a small gap between the mini blinds and the window case. Could he see me beside the bed, or would I be hidden if I stayed low?

I stayed low and crawled on hands and knees to the door, reached one arm up, and slowly turned the knob. *God, please don't let him see the door opening. Please don't let him see me.*

As soon as it was cracked wide enough, I slipped into the hallway, stood up, and burst through my parents' door without knocking. "He's outside my window!"

Dad leapt out of bed right as his eyes popped open, and in three long-legged strides, he was in my bedroom flipping on the light. One more leap and he was across the room, yanking up the mini blinds as Mom rushed in. Dad saw his own reflection in the glass until Mom flipped the light back off. He squinted into the dark outside scanning for any movement, but there was nothing.

He slipped his shoes on and patrolled outside for a while, but he didn't find anyone, which wasn't unusual for these nighttime visits.

My parents went back to bed. This was business as usual for them—had been for three months. I bunched up the comforter and carried it to the couch. I couldn't sleep in that room. I lay down on the couch in the living room where there weren't any blinds, only lacy curtain panels between whatever might be hiding in the dark and me. I kept my eyes on the windows.

Ray might have come to kill me. Dad might have scared him off. Or it could have been an animal walking through the yard. It even could have been my adrenaline-soaked imagination. He might not have come *this night*, but he was coming. I wasn't ready to die, but I was ready to finish this.

I was done letting my parents cage me up and keep me in Conway, as if that somehow made us all safer. I was done waiting around for the inevitable phone call that said my family had been in a terrible accident. I was done playing Ray's game.

CHAPTER TWENTY-TWO

Mom and Angela slept while I sat up on the living room couch, watching *South Park* reruns and guarding our home with a blunt chef's knife. Dad had run off to the apartment above Radio Shack for the night, but that was my fault.

Three days after heading back to campus, I came home again and announced I'd dropped out of school. Mom kept telling me they couldn't leave Arkansas because I'd be there alone, and I couldn't leave Arkansas with them because I was in college, and I couldn't leave college without losing my scholarship. Now we could all leave because I'd traded in my four-year scholarship for an escape route for all of us. There were no more excuses to hide behind.

I didn't want to leave. Pine Creek was my home, and all my friends lived along a trail from Little Rock to Pine Creek, but what good are friends when your family's dead? When *you're* dead? When survival is your main priority, you're willing to give up anything.

At least *my* version paints me as a hero, willing to make self-sacrificial choices for the good of her family. To my parents, I'd made an impulsive and selfish choice, dropping out of school without talking it over with them, and then showing up unannounced, demanding we all start packing. At the time, I didn't appreciate that my family felt like they were in more danger if I was in the house.

Dad wasn't ready to move yet. He was still trying to work with the police to get Ray under control. If we left, Dad would be abandoning the church he'd pastored for the last four years and leaving the congregation without a pastor. That meant Elmer would run the church. Since Elmer couldn't even bring himself to rid the church of a man like Ray, what sort of position would that leave the congregation we loved in?

And where could we even go? Texas? Ray knew we had family in Texas. It was the first place he'd look.

And how could we afford to go? We didn't own the parsonage, so we couldn't sell our house. Churches are slow about hiring new pastors, so it wasn't like Dad could just step out of this church and into a new job within a few days. With no place to go, and no source of income, we were stuck.

Dad needed some space to think, so he grabbed some stuff and headed out to the apartment. I don't remember what I said to that, but I'm sure I made some sort of hateful comment about abandonment or finding our burned corpses in the morning as he slammed the front door on his way out.

I'd seen Dad jump down a dozen bleachers in a split second when he saw some kid shove my cousin at a football game. He'd outrun a spooked horse while I held onto the saddle horn and screamed. He was the kind of person you'd read about lifting a car off his kid. But he couldn't lift Ray off us. Or maybe he just *wouldn't* because Jesus said not to. I couldn't tell.

Dropping out without discussing it with my parents first was an impulsive move, but at least it was a move. Passively waiting around for Ray's next scare tactic was sucking all the color out of my life. All my emotions had numbed down, just so I could get through each day, and I felt like I was starting to lose myself. Even if Ray didn't physically kill me, he was still killing part of me. I had to do something to fight back and take control of my life. There weren't many things I had control of, but my enrollment status was one of them.

That night, I kept the lights off and the TV volume low so I could hear Ray break in, and so Mom wouldn't hear *South Park* through her bedroom wall and holler at me to turn it off because she didn't allow that kind of garbage in her house. Technically, we weren't even supposed to watch *The Simpsons*.

I started eyeing the phone around midnight. How quickly could I jump off the couch, run past the dining room table, and dial 911 if he broke in? How long would it take the police to respond?

Too long.

TV light flickered reassuringly off the knife on the end table as some bastards killed Kenny. Every few minutes, my swept eyes across the lace-covered windows and the windowed front door. No bearded faces stared back at me. Yet.

Dad's van was gone. The white station wagon I'd

been driving was in the parking lot out front. If Ray was watching the house, he'd know this was the night to make his move. He might have been crazy, but he wasn't stupid. He'd know this would be his best shot.

I hoped he was coming. I wanted to see the surprise on his face when he saw I had a knife. I wanted to slice his smug smirk right off. I wouldn't even get in trouble for it. Self-defense, they'd say. Brave girl, going up against a grown man like that. Saved her whole family. What a hero.

The whole church would be in an uproar. Elmer would backpedal and claim he'd been suspicious of Ray all along. Jackie would bawl crocodile tears and beg me to forgive her. Ben would cry real tears, knowing I never could forgive his lack of support. Mike and Rhonda would be interviewed by a TV news crew from Little Rock, that couple who talks about how well they thought they knew the criminal and how he'd fooled so many people, and thank God I'd had the presence of mind to take care of him before he hurt anyone else.

Mom and Angela might be a little traumatized after seeing his dead body and all the blood. Maybe I could kill him quietly enough that I wouldn't wake Angela up. She was all the way across the house. Mom would hear the commotion and come running, but she'd get over it more easily than Angela would. Even though she preached nonviolence at me, I figured she'd secretly be relieved I'd taken care of it.

Dad wouldn't be happy, but he'd be so overcome with guilt about leaving us alone all night that he wouldn't come down on me. Anyway, we both knew the whole pacifism thing didn't come easily to me.

I rehearsed scenarios in my head. If he climbed through my bedroom window again, I'd slip down the hall and stab him in the back. If he walked through the front door, I couldn't decide if I should leap up and go wild slashing at him or if I should pretend to cower on the couch until he came close enough to grab me, and then go wild slashing at him.

A thump sounded down the hall, and I froze to listen.

Mom's door opened, the hall light turned on, and the bathroom door squeaked shut. I set a throw pillow over the knife and hit the previous channel button on the remote.

Mom walked out of the bathroom and hovered right outside the hall. "How late you staying up?" she asked.

"Late. I can't sleep."

She sighed. "I'm having a hard time sleeping too."

I told her I'd wake her up if I went to bed, and that sounded like a good enough plan to her. As soon as her door clicked shut, I switched back to Comedy Central.

All night I sat beside the knife I was sure would be enough to keep us safe. When the windows turned gray, I felt safe enough to put the knife back into its block, then went to my room and crashed, fully clothed, onto my bed to catch a little sleep.

Even though it was mid-October, the sun was out full blast a few hours later, and the day was warm enough for a T-shirt. Dad had come home while I napped. I snuck past the kitchen where Mom and Dad were hashing things out and walked next door to the church.

A church key hung off a peg in the kitchen, but I didn't bother grabbing it on my way out. Everyone knew you didn't need a key to get into the church. You just had to grip the side window with your fingertips and push it up until you could slide a finger under the crack, then hoist the window the rest of the way up with your palm. Reach an arm through and snake it around until you hit the doorknob to the left of the window. Click the lock and walk on in.

The window slammed back down, and I walked into the sanctuary I hadn't stepped foot in for almost three months. There was no way it could ever feel unfamiliar, though. I'd spent about as much time in the church as I'd spent in the parsonage.

It was cooler and dimmer in the sanctuary than outside in the sun. I walked down the main aisle and checked my old pew, just to make sure nothing was sitting there again. It was empty, so I circled back to the front and sat down at the upright piano to plunk out a clumsy melody from the open hymnal. Each slow note echoed in the cold church.

After a while, I gave up on the piano and walked past all the pews toward the foyer. Nothing new had been posted on the bulletin board. Every sheet of paper was tacked up in the same spot, like a slap in the face. I was

Act Normal

living in a twister these people had helped create, but not one pushpin was out of place.

A folded, white sheet of paper sat in my family's church mailbox, even though all the other mailboxes were empty. It reminded me of Mom's favorite "God provides" story from when Dad was in seminary and money was extra tight. Growing up, Angela and I always got new dresses for Easter. That year, we found some frilly dresses on a clearance rack, and two of them fit us perfectly. Mom had $20 on her, enough to buy both dresses, but not enough left over to tithe at church on Sunday. She told us to put the dresses back, and when Sunday morning rolled around, she put the $20 bill into the offering plate as it went by. After church, she grabbed the newsletter and other papers out of our church mailbox and found an envelope. Inside was $50 and a note that said, "Thought you could use this." The next day, we got our dresses.

I reached out and grabbed the paper, figuring it was something like that. At best, it was a Bible verse someone thought would give my parents some hope and encouragement. At worst, it was some note about maintenance around the church, like the men's room toilet was broken or someone was complaining about the front doors being dirty.

The folds slid against one other, and the sheet crinkled as I straightened the creases. It was unnervingly loud in the silent sanctuary. An address label had been peeled off a piece of mail and glued to the page: my name, followed by our street address. Under that was an address label with Mom's name on it.

Below our names was an obituary cut out of the *Pine Creek News* and glued down. He must have cut my name out of a lot of envelopes because *Kristy* was glued over every mention of the dead person's name. Over and over. I would be buried in the Eastrun Cemetery, immediately following my funeral.

My chest seized up like someone had blown the hatch on the sanctuary and voided all the oxygen. This wasn't Ray doing something bizarre like drawing an eye and leaving it up to us to interpret how far he'd take things. There was no room for interpretation here. I was dead.

A rational person would realize what scratched out brides and a fire meant, but it's hard to be objective when you're living in the middle of all that. There were times when I understood where we might be headed, but most of the time I thought Ray just wanted to scare me. We tend to believe what we want to believe, and I didn't want to believe someone was planning my murder.

Because, if that was true, I had to ask why. A rational person expects rational explanations. People don't just up and murder their pastor's daughter for no good reason. I must have done *something* to egg him on. I shouldn't have been up front performing all those skits and drawing attention to myself. I shouldn't have let Ben put his arm around me during worship services. I shouldn't have worn shorts while working on the church addition.

It was easier to believe we were overreacting. Ray just had a little crush on me, and he was mad because I didn't want to be with him. Sometimes men got jealous and acted out a little. He'd get over it soon and everything would calm down. Women only got murdered in movies, not in real life.

Except it *does* happen in real life, and Ray had just promised it would. Setting a small fire wasn't his climax. That was just a preview.

My eyes snapped up to the stairs on my right. Was he up there in the little room off the bell tower right now? My heart hammered as I turned around to stare at the door to the Fellowship Hall, another possible hiding spot. I should have checked the whole building first. I shouldn't have come into the church alone.

My plan was to creep back out of the church, but two tip-toes in, I panicked and broke into a full run. I ran away from the foyer where Ben had shown me, if he turned his hand upside down, the lines in our palms matched our last initials. I ran down the aisle I was supposed to parade down in a white dress, past the stage where I'd performed skits with my youth group, and through the side door everyone knew how to break into.

CHAPTER TWENTY-THREE

Angela was hoarding all the newspaper for her Star Trek figurines, so I stormed into her bedroom to stake my claim on half of it. "Whatever," she said, "I'm almost done anyway."

The only thing left on her long purple shelf was a model of the *Enterprise*. Everything else had already been carefully wrapped and stacked into the cardboard box on her bed. Her favorite doll, a Cabbage Patch preemie that six-year-old Angela had named Roseanna, sat on top of the mummified *Enterprise* crew and peeked over the edge of the box at me.

I propped myself up against the wall and watched her gently lay Roseanna down and tape the box shut. "Where were you this morning?" I asked.

Mom had pulled her out of school days ago, but Angela had mysteriously vanished for a few hours earlier. She smirked. "Kelly called to tell me where they were taking the class picture today, so I snuck in."

"You *should* be in the class picture."

"I *should* be doing a lot of things."

I stared at her as she stood on an uneven chair and reached toward the *Enterprise*. She was right. She should get to go to her senior prom and graduate with the kids

Act Normal

she'd gone to school with since eighth grade, but she couldn't because we had to move. Because of me.

I tossed the newspaper back onto her bed. I'd find something else to wrap my jewelry box with. I didn't want to be responsible for crushing the Federation's flagship.

The obituary was the last straw for Dad. He made some phone calls that afternoon to get advice. One of the last calls was to his longtime friend, DeRoy, from Indiana. "Get them out of there," DeRoy said. He said we could move in with him until we figured out what to do next, but we had to leave Arkansas.

We packed in secret. If word got to Ray that we were getting ready to run for it, well, we had a pretty good idea what Ray would do.

On Sunday morning, the four of us walked into church together. Dad stationed himself up front while Mom, Angela, and I went to sit down. I headed toward my regular pew, but Angela stopped me. "Not there," she said before steering me into the second pew from the back, right in front of the pew where all my friends from youth group—including Daniel and Ben—were already sitting. Later, she told me she'd asked them all to sit there as a buffer so Ray couldn't sneak up behind me.

As the rest of the church members—including Ray—filtered in, I scowled like I'd never scowled before. I wasn't going to sit there and pretend everything was OK just so everyone else would feel more comfortable.

Dad stood behind the pulpit and said, "I need to share something with you this morning. This is my last Sunday preaching."

A couple of ladies gasped. I'm not sure if they were really surprised or if they just thought the proper thing to do when a pastor quits is act horrified. Dad ignored them and went on with, "We're moving in two weeks, and I think you need to know why."

Angela and I turned to one another and raised our eyebrows. *Two weeks?* We were leaving in a few days. Our dad, the man who'd told us he wouldn't have lied to the Nazis if he had a Jewish family hidden in the basement because lying is a sin and he'd trust in God's protection, had just lied from the pulpit.

Dad said we were being harassed, which was a nice, diplomatic way of putting it. He cautiously walked them through the past three months, never once slipping up and tossing out the name so many of the church members were foaming at the mouths to get. A situation like this was a small-town gossip's dream, and naming Ray would only fuel the idea that my family had unfairly targeted him. If we pointed to Ray, *he* would become the victim. We'd already seen that happen with Ben's family.

When Dad got to the part about me finding my underwear in the church, the congregation swiveled around in their pews to stare at me and wonder what kind of underwear it had been. Something slutty, obviously, or else this mystery harasser wouldn't be

Act Normal

bothering me.

The overhead projector hummed on, and Dad pulled the screen down from the ceiling so it hid the wooden cross that hung above the altar. Copies of underlined Bible pages appeared. Verses about my breasts and nakedness and prostitution were blown up big enough for the blindest congregant to read. My silent church family stared up at God's projected word and wondered what awful thing I'd done to justify those underlined passages.

Dad told them about the fire, and I expected some gasps at that point, but there weren't any. I also would've thought people who'd known my family for over four years would leap straight out of their pews and offer to pay for an alarm system on the parsonage or take shifts driving by the house at night or let us crash with them for a while until we got everything sorted out. But they just sat there, passively taking it all in. Because *they* weren't the ones doing these things to us, so what responsibility did they have to fix it?

To be fair, aside from the church council and a handful of other members, most people that morning were probably hearing about it for the first time. But still. Where was all that righteous indignation I saw anytime someone mentioned teaching school kids about evolution? I was sure murder threats trumped Darwin.

When I glanced at Angela again, she was trying to stop crying. On the other side of her, Mom sat with the hardest expression I'd ever seen on her face. She'd been plenty angry before, but this was the closest I think she ever got to full-on rage. I wondered if that was how I looked to everyone and tried to soften my expression a little, but my jaw was locked up tight. I was sure Angela looked way more sympathetic than either of us. Nobody feels sorry for an angry woman.

Dad replaced the Bible verses with a copy of the obituary. Angela shifted a little, then reached over and grabbed my hand so tightly I was sure she'd bruise me. She told me later she'd peeked across the aisle at Ray and saw him smiling at me.

The obituary stayed up as Dad explained why we had to leave. It wasn't safe to stay. He started getting choked up when he said, even though he had an obligation to the church, his family came first. I thought about John, my parents' friend from Indiana whose donation had started our building fund. When we moved from Indiana to work with the Mennonites in Oklahoma, John had hung back after Sunday night church service to give Dad some advice. "Remember," he'd said, as he held three fingers up and named them, "God first. Family second. Church third." It'd confused me at the time, but I understood now. Serving a church wasn't always the same thing as serving God.

Our church service ended abruptly when Dad shut off the overhead and stepped away from the pulpit. No hymns. No closing prayer. No dismissing us with, "Go in peace."

Before I could stand up, Jackie was at my side with a hand on my shoulder. She leaned down to face level and said, loud enough for everyone to hear, "I'll pray you

Act Normal

find out who's really doing all this."

It's possible I beat Mom's rage face for a minute there because she yanked her hand off like I'd singed her, and backed away quickly. I stood up, and Mike nearly knocked me over as he threw an arm around my shoulder and squeezed. "Y'all are just precious," he said with a thick voice, tears starting up.

I flung his arm off and turned my back on him. What right did he have to cry about it? What was this costing *him*? He was too busy defending Ray to ever check on me or offer any real help. He'd kept Ray's keys at night to prove Ray was innocent and save *him*, not me. What had anyone in this church done to show me I was precious? You protect what's precious to you. I wasn't precious. I was a burnt offering to their false idol.

Angela and I switched places after that so I was wedged between my sister and mother. Nobody could get to me without going past Angela first. Somehow, she stopped anyone else from reaching me. Maybe they were more comfortable squeezing her shoulder and whispering lies they wished were true into her ear instead of mine.

Ben stood quietly, inches from me, and stared at the floor while people moved around us. I wondered if any rumors had gotten back to him about what—and who— I'd been doing in Conway.

After everyone else had cleared out of the sanctuary, he moved a step closer to me and asked, "You going too?"

It was a ridiculous question, and I was so strung out

on stress and insomnia that I laughed before recovering enough to say, "Moving's pointless if I don't go too."

He used to smile and tease me about how easy it was to make me laugh, but his lips didn't flutter even for a second. Instead, his face broke, and he didn't even try to stop the tears that fell and landed on the pew between us. I should have cried too, but the tears didn't come. I'd put so much effort into numbing myself to push through all the anxiety and loneliness and rage that grief barely even registered.

Even if I didn't have the luxury of being able to access my own grief, I could appreciate his. I closed the gap between us and wrapped my arms around his neck. He hugged me back, and I whispered, "I know," into his ear as he cried, though I wasn't sure exactly what it was I knew. Just in time, I caught myself before tilting my head to kiss his cheek. We couldn't do that sort of thing anymore.

Dad walked back into the sanctuary. We released each other, and I shot an irritated look Dad's way for interrupting our good-bye. "We didn't know where you were," he said, which really meant, *We couldn't find you in the house, so we thought Ray might have kidnapped you.*

"Just give me a minute," I told him.

He walked back out, and Ben wiped his hands across his face. I took a step back to give him room to walk past me and out the door, but he didn't move.

"I'm going now," I announced, because I didn't know what else to say.

He nodded and followed me to the side door. I

turned back to him in the parking lot, gave him a smile and said, "Good-bye."

He didn't smile back, but stared at me for one last minute and looked like he was going to say something. When he didn't speak up, I turned and headed down the sidewalk to the parsonage. I watched out the living room window as his truck pulled out of the parking lot.

Angela stepped up beside me as his truck disappeared behind a wall of trees. "What'd he say?" she asked.

"Nothing."

Part Two

**DECEMBER 1999
MIDDLEBURY, INDIANA**

How can we sing the songs of the LORD while in a foreign land?

– Psalm 137:4

*What has been will be again,
what has been done will be done again;
there is nothing new under the sun.*

– Ecclesiastes 1:9

CHAPTER TWENTY-FOUR

Holy crap. Now that is some serious cleavage. I turned sideways in the tiny dressing room and checked out my profile again. For some reason, the good Lord created me with wide hips and almost nothing up top to balance them out, which I'd always been self-conscious about. But something about the way that tight, black tank top squeezed everything together changed all that. How could I *not* buy a miraculous, breast-growing tank top? I *deserved* a breast-growing tank top.

The real problem was I hadn't found it on the clearance rack. I was wearing a full-priced tank top and velvet skirt when I was supposed to be scouring clearance sales with Mom, trying to find a few Christmas presents so we'd have *something* under the tree. I just wanted to try the outfit on for fun, but it's not actually all that fun when you desperately want something you can't have.

Two months earlier, I'd moved into an upstairs bedroom at DeRoy's. Angela and I shared a double bed in a room with pink-flowered wallpaper and a slanted roof I constantly bumped my head on. Angela only lasted a week there before moving to Goshen to live with our old pastor and his wife. Mom and Dad had enrolled her in a small Christian school in Goshen, and living with them made the commute easier for her. She had a hard time adjusting to a new school, full of straight-laced Mennonite kids, especially after coming out of the nightmare she'd just moved out of. A month into our exile, she and Daniel broke up over the phone, though they kept in touch.

Daniel was one of the only people who knew where we were. On the day we moved, I'd called one of my best friends, Louise, to tell her good-bye and that I was moving to Indiana. But I didn't even give her the name of the town I was moving to. Only Daniel and one of Dad's friends had our address, so he could forward any mail. Both of them were sworn to secrecy. Dad had told our church we were leaving, but he hadn't told them where we were going. And because Ben's family had been so supportive of Ray, it hadn't even been safe for me to tell Ben.

From the perspective of most of the people we knew in Pine Creek, my family just disappeared one day. Years later, one of Angela's classmates found her on MySpace and sent a message to tell her how excited she was to see Angela on there. Because when Angela stopped showing up to school and our whole family dropped off the face of the earth, the rumor was we'd all been murdered.

It's hard to pull off a disappearing act. Most people wouldn't be able to do it. If Dad hadn't just happened to have a single friend who owned a three-bedroom house, we wouldn't have had anywhere to go. How can you just up and move when you don't have a job or a house to move into?

We had a house, at least temporarily, but jobs were harder to find and money was a problem. Mom noticed a help wanted sign while driving through Middlebury a few days after we moved. She strode into the main office and got hired on the spot. She worked as a seamstress, making drapes for RVs. A couple of days later, they hired me as a fabric cutter because it doesn't really take a lot of skill to cut a straight line. Mom's chronic pain flared up so badly she had to quit, but I'd have stuck it out if I hadn't gotten into a thumb-wrestling match with a fabric-cutting saw.

Losing the tip of my right thumb wasn't a total loss, though. The worker's compensation checks sure helped while we were all unemployed, and I was still technically on the payroll for the Christmas bonus, which was an extra $200 we hadn't expected. I should have deposited it into Mom and Dad's bank account along with the worker's comp check, but I just couldn't do it. I was tired of being practical and responsible. When I spotted the extra check, I held it up for Mom to see and said, "Let's go Christmas shopping."

I wanted to do something frivolous, like dig our fake Christmas tree out of DeRoy's barn and buy a few presents to stick under it. I was counting on Christmas to pull me out of the funk I'd been in since crossing the Arkansas state line. I'd been shut up at DeRoy's for almost two months. Even if my right hand hadn't been splinted and bandaged up, I had nowhere to go. I thought about looking up my two friends from junior high, but they'd ask what I'd been up to, and how could I answer a question like that? Oh, just running from a stalker who wants to kill me. You know. The usual.

It wasn't hard to isolate myself. Sometimes Dad worked temp jobs, which took him out of the house. He put together cardboard boxes and spent some early winter weeks shingling a roof. When he wasn't working, he and DeRoy put together jigsaw puzzles. A knee-high stack of puzzle boxes ran along the perimeter of the front room. A thousand pieces. Five thousand pieces. Duck ponds and suspension bridges. Famous paintings and pastoral scenes. They found them at thrift shops for five and ten cents, and they never knew if all the pieces were there until the puzzle was done.

We didn't talk about Ray. At least I never did. I'd felt a gulf between me and everyone else since I first moved to UCA, and it was even worse now. They were the ones who'd lived through Ray's craziness every day. They had been in danger more often than I'd been. They were justified in grieving their losses. But I wasn't. What right did I have to grieve for a church that didn't want me? For a boy who didn't love me? How could I tell them how homesick I was when they gave up that same home because of me?

Ray's name only came up once, about a month after we left. Dad called his friend from Radio Shack and found out Ray had stopped by the store, claiming Dad had lent him some books and he wanted to mail them back, so could he get our new address? When Dad's friend offered to mail the books for him, Ray changed his story and said the books *didn't* need to come back to Dad.

Usually, I only thought about Ray at night. I was pretty sure he didn't know where I was, but I couldn't be absolutely positive. I told myself I was on the second floor and nobody could scale the sheer wall to get to my bedroom window, but then ladders whirled through my mind, so I'd turn my laptop on and start reading to calm down.

Dad splurged on a dial-up Internet connection, which was the only thing that kept me a little sane while my thumb healed. I discovered fanfiction, which I loaded onto a floppy disk on the desktop downstairs and carried upstairs to read on my laptop. Some of the stories were pretty good. Some of them were barely decipherable. It didn't matter. As long as I was reading, I wasn't thinking.

It took some practice, but I trained myself to hit the space bar with my left thumb, to spare my injured right thumb, and started to write my own fanfiction. Familiar characters dropped into my own scenarios to see how things would play out. Maybe it was the painkillers I was taking for my thumb, but everyone got traumatized in my stories.

I found some drawing tutorials online and managed to balance a pencil along the edge of my splint. My comic book heroine was a young woman with an orphaned little sister she had to take care of. None of the other heroes paid much attention to her because they thought she had the lamest power ever—the power of memory—but that was only because they didn't understand it.

She could remember everything she'd ever seen, which came in handy while problem-solving. Plus, she could force other people to relive any of their memories. Imagine being forced to relive your most traumatic memories over and over again. Batman pisses her off? Guess who gets to experience his parents' murder on a loop?

Everything I owned was locked up in DeRoy's barn. All I brought into the house was my laptop, one suitcase, and one garbage bag full of clothes. I couldn't bring myself to hang anything up in the closet. I'd wash my clothes, then return them to the black garbage bag.

We were technically homeless, and I was getting dressed out of a garbage bag every morning. It was why I wanted that new outfit so badly. It was the sort of outfit a normal girl would wear. The kind of girl who still had a home and a scholarship. The kind of girl who didn't attract creepy, older men, but kind, young, smart, and handsome men.

I'd never had to attract anyone before. Ben met me when I was fourteen (when I definitely did not have anything a black tank top could squeeze upward) and I hadn't done anything to get his attention. I was just sort of *there* all the time, so maybe I grew on him. And Matt? We'd gone to school together for a while, so that was probably the same thing.

I wasn't ready to dive into a new relationship yet, but I'd be ready eventually, and I didn't want to hang around some guy's peripheral vision for two years before he noticed I was standing there. That meant I had to put out a little effort to get the right guy's attention. Well, everyone knew breasts got attention. Not *my* breasts, usually, but breasts in general.

Dad had talked me into enrolling at a small Mennonite college for the winter semester. There was a chance I'd meet someone there. Maybe I'd be walking through campus with my awesome black tank top on, and some really smart, funny, nice guy would notice me. Sure, at first it'd be all about my brand-new cleavage, but once he got to know me, he'd see past my breasts and into my heart. I was sure that was how it worked.

I had to buy the tank top. What was $30 compared to my future romantic happiness?

CHAPTER TWENTY-FIVE

Dad visited different churches every week. One Sunday, I woke up early and tagged along. I wore a pink shirt and my nicest pleated skirt. Other than the bright-blue splint on my right thumb, I looked pretty dang normal.

But when I sat in the pew I felt like a phony. I didn't belong there with those good Christians. I was sitting there pretending to be one of them when I knew I wasn't. I hated people, and I couldn't be a Christian if I hated people. I hated Ray. I hated Jackie. I hated Elmer. I hated Mike. I even hated Ben. I hated them all so much because I should have been sitting in a pew with *them* that morning, not in some church in Indiana with a bunch of people I didn't know who sang songs I'd never heard of before and who had their worship service all out of order.

For a while after we moved in with DeRoy, time and distance didn't make much sense to me. Everything happened so fast that it was hard for my brain to catch up and remember this was where we lived now. Sometimes I got the feeling that all I had to do was hop in the car and drive down the road a few miles to get back home, where I could call Ben and ask if he wanted to see a movie. Sometimes it felt like I'd always lived in the slant-ceilinged room at DeRoy's. Nothing came before that and nothing would ever come after.

But it wasn't always depressing. Angela would come over sometimes and we'd check out old musicals from the library, and then we'd go around singing at each other the rest of the day. She took a creative writing class, and I helped her write a goofy poem about how her sister was so dumb she cut off her thumb.

On New Year's Eve 1999, I sat on the couch next to Dad and waited for the ball to drop on DeRoy's tiny TV. I poked Dad's arm, and he glanced up from his book. "What'll we do if all the lights go off at midnight?"

A decent portion of our congregation in Arkansas had been in a panic over the Y2K bug for the past couple of years. They thought we were crazy for not hoarding toilet paper and ammunition. It took Dad all of five minutes to fix our family computer, so I was reasonably confident that NASA could handle theirs.

Dad frowned at me. "All our neighbors are Amish. I think we'll be OK."

He went back to his book, and I thought about how disappointed all the preppers would be around 12:05 a.m. But, on the off chance we were wrong, and all the hoarders were right, what *would* happen to us?

Dad was onto something. We were in the perfect place if the power grid went down and the government collapsed. The Amish knew how to live off the land, and they didn't use electricity, anyway. They'd help us out. Besides, it wasn't like they had any weapons to defend their resources, so it'd be pretty easy to raid them if I had to.

I wouldn't mind defending them, though. Most of the people in the area were Mennonites or Amish, so they'd need someone to defend them if things got really bad. Maybe I could form some sort of post-apocalyptic community of pacifists. They'd grow the food and I'd hold onto the guns.

Years later, when all the stockpiles would have run out, we'd get an influx of refugees from the south. Maybe a group from northern Arkansas would hear about the Promised Land in Indiana where people are prospering under the wise leadership of their gun-toting president. They'd show up at the gates, and I'd stand on the other side of the fence and watch their shocked faces. I'd shake my head and bar them from the land of milk and honey and whoopie pies. They'd be sorry then. They'd know what it felt like to be forced out into the wilderness.

The ball dropped and the lights stayed on.

CHAPTER TWENTY-SIX

Dad thought I'd never go back to school if I didn't go back right away, so he drove me to a nearby Mennonite college to sign loan papers I didn't fully understand. In January, I moved into the dorms.

At first I was thrilled to be out of DeRoy's house. I was starved for human contact by then, and maybe that's why most of the other students steered clear of me. I probably gave off some kind of desperate, damaged, non-ethnically Mennonite pheromone that warned them off.

It wasn't that people weren't nice. They were painfully nice. And polite and reserved and gentle and a whole bunch of other things I've never been accused of being. The only girl who invited me to do anything with her was a girl from Mexico who lived a few doors down. I sat on her dorm floor to watch Spanish soaps twice that semester. I was practically an international student too, from the feral lands to the south, where people chewed tobacco, watched NASCAR, and wouldn't recognize hymn 606 if it bit 'em on the ass.

Most of the time, I sat by myself in the common room between the male and female dorm wings because that's where the TV was. It's where I met J.R.

I was sitting on a threadbare couch in the dorm common room one night, reading about Watergate, when two boys strolled through.

"You're hot!"

My head shot up so fast the tall, red-headed boy still had his hands cupped around his grinning mouth. The other boy, shorter and broader than the one who'd yelled, just stared at me.

I had to respond. Nobody had ever just waltzed in and yelled something like that at me before, but I'd seen it happen to other girls often enough to know he'd take a non-response as a challenge, and I needed him to go away so I could study.

"I know," I said, like I couldn't believe he'd made such an obvious comment, then turned my head back down to my book.

He got a little flustered that I hadn't either thanked him or flipped him off. His shorter friend told him, "Come on, don't do that to girls," and dragged him through the door.

One and a half chapters later, the short boy came back and introduced himself as J.R. He apologized for his friend, and we spent the next few hours talking. He wanted to know where my southern drawl came from, and since he seemed genuinely interested, that led to a summarized version of my life story. I told him I'd left Arkansas to get away from a stalker, who happened to be a member of my old church. He said he was glad I'd gotten away. It was a safe campus, and people looked out for one another here, so I shouldn't be scared.

When he asked about a boyfriend, I told him I'd broken off an engagement and wanted to stay single until I sorted out all my issues. It didn't seem fair to drag anyone else down under that weight. He thought that sounded real mature.

We started hanging out a lot after that. It was nice to have someone to eat lunch with and watch TV with in the evenings. He teased me about skipping chapel—a graduation requirement—so I grudgingly went with him. It wasn't as bad when I had someone to sit next to, but some of the prayers and sermons I heard there sent a pang of anxiety straight through me.

It hurt to sit through those chapel services and hear people quote supposedly inspirational Bible verses about trials and tribulations when they'd probably never been through anything worse than a failed test. It hurt to hear those kids talk about how much God loved everyone when it didn't feel like he cared about me at all. It hurt to sing songs about feeling the presence of God when I didn't feel a damn thing.

Attending chapel brought on a soul-squeezing sort of pain, like I was intentionally hurting myself, just by forcing myself to sit through the service. J.R. suggested I tag along to a Bible study group he was in. He said it might be a good way to get back into the swing of things.

The Bible study leader was a scrawny guy with wire-rimmed glasses and a patient attitude. He and J.R. spent most of my first meeting going round and round about context while the rest of the small group mostly kept quiet. J.R. figured you could pluck any old verse out of the Bible and apply it to your life. Our Bible study leader thought you needed to read the surrounding verses to keep everything in context. I spent the hour listening and absorbing, but not offering any of my own opinions until the week after when I did chime in with a couple of comments.

I thought J.R. might be right. It might be a nice, safe way of dipping my toe back in. I'd done some things over the past few months I wasn't exactly proud of, but I could be redeemed. I could get back that joy I used to have in being a part of a Christian community. I could belong again. Maybe J.R. and his group could Moses me back into the Promised Land.

When I went back to DeRoy's for a weekend, I dug around in the garage and pulled my pink Bible out of a hastily packed box. A year before, I'd have been horrified at the thought of neglecting my Bible for months, but I hadn't cracked it open since right before I broke up with Ben. With all the hate in my heart and the pot I was smoking and that whole one-night and one-morning stand thing, I didn't feel worthy of reading God's word. But I wasn't doing anything wrong *now*, so maybe it was OK to dive back in.

I still had trouble sleeping at night, which made things tough for my roommate, so I spared her my desk lamp by slipping out to the common room late at night to read my Bible when I couldn't sleep. I read my way back through Matthew, and little zings of doubt hit me. Most Christians I'd known weren't anything like what Jesus said they should be. They'd help people, but only when it was convenient or didn't cost them too much. And, oh, did they ever love to judge. Well, they loved to judge *me*, at least. Ray, not so much.

Then again, according to the book of Matthew, I wasn't much of a Christian either. Jesus said I should turn the other cheek and love my enemies, but I didn't want to do that. I wanted them all to suffer as much as I had.

Now that I'd had a few months' reprieve from Ray, I had time to think about what came next. I should have been worried about him finding some other girl to target and possibly even murder, but I was too busy being bitter over the fact that he'd gotten away with what he'd done to *me*.

I daydreamed about driving down to Pine Creek and putting up fliers all over town, telling everyone what he'd done. Or putting up a website and telling the whole story there, which I thought was a great idea since a website had gotten me in trouble with the church council last time.

The Bible said not to retaliate, but it didn't exactly tell me where the line between justice and retaliation was. There was a little consolation waiting for me in Matthew 18, though.

If anyone causes one of these little ones—those who believe in me—to stumble, it would be better for them to have a large millstone hung around their neck and to be drowned in the depths of the sea. Woe to the world because of the things that cause people to stumble! Such things must come, but woe to the person through whom they come!

I saw a millstone once. The mental image of that enormous chunk of rock hanging off Ray's neck, dragging him to the bottom of the ocean was more satisfying than I'd like to admit. And in my imagination, that millstone had ropes tied around it and the other ends of those ropes were wrapped around the ankles of every church council member who'd let him get away with hurting me. Ray dragged them down into the dark with him while they wept and gnashed their teeth.

CHAPTER TWENTY-SEVEN

Sometimes Dad drove by campus and picked me up on his way to one of the Mennonite churches he visited. At least they called themselves a church. I wasn't totally sure what they were. The group would meet on Saturday nights, and instead of listening to a sermon we'd all sit in a circle on the floor and rap about scripture. That's what *they'd* do, anyway. I'd sit silently and count how many people wore sandals in the middle of winter (most of them, by the way).

Then we'd all go into the other room where we'd find round tables set up with baskets of bread, and older women who'd come by with bowls of soup and cups of grape juice. We'd eat our fellowship meal together, and I'd eavesdrop on the people around me. This guy boasted about a protest he was going to. That guy talked about his mission trip.

I mostly went for the free food. The people there were nice, and not quite as squeaky clean as the kids on campus, but they still seemed to have sanded down all their splinters. They were good, and that meant I didn't fit.

But I kept going because I used to love going to church, and I missed that connection. I remembered what it felt like to sing out to God with people I loved. I wanted to rebuild and tap into that joy I'd had in my faith again.

Building a new family of Christians is tough when you're having a hard time trusting Christians, though. I wanted to believe those people meant what they said, but how could I know? They talked about helping people, and they went to protests, and fed the community, but if something difficult came up—something that required a *real* sacrifice—what would happen then? Would they tend Christ's sheep or let the wolves gnaw on them?

Some of the people there tried to talk to me. I can't say they didn't try to reach out. It's just hard to reach back sometimes, especially when reaching out means letting go.

I was more comfortable in J.R.'s weekly Bible Study group. I'd always been under the impression that anyone could read any part of the Bible and understand it just fine, without any outside help, but our group leader kept talking about understanding the history and culture of the people who wrote it all down. I'd also thought of the Bible as one big book God dictated to human secretaries who faithfully wrote it down, word for word. I didn't know that each book had been written at different points in time, in different locations, and under different

Act Normal

circumstances. That knowledge opened up all sorts of interesting and, frankly, frightening possibilities.

J.R. took everything in the Bible literally. He called it the "plain reading" of scripture. If Genesis said God created the world in six days, then God created the world in exactly six days. End of story. But our group leader wasn't so set on that, and neither were most of the other group members, which absolutely blew my freakin' mind. Some people thought parts of the Bible weren't literal, which sent J.R. into a tizzy because if you don't take it all literally, how do you know which parts to throw out and which to keep? Which was exactly what I wanted to know. I couldn't imagine a Christian faith built on such a sandy foundation.

Still, the group leader seemed smart, and he seemed to know his Bible too. I kept meaning to catch him after group and talk to him without everyone else around, but J.R. always hung back when I did, and he'd dominate any conversation I tried to have, so that never worked out.

After a couple of months on campus, J.R. was still my only friend. I was thankful to have someone to talk to. He didn't know every gory detail, but he knew the basics of what I'd been through, and he never judged me for being skittish about religion.

He owned a large VHS collection, so we spent most evenings in the common room watching whatever movie he picked out for us. Usually, I'd fall asleep toward the end of the movie. Insomnia was still an issue, and I slept better with someone around who could give a shout if some long-bearded hippie leapt through the window and tried to set me on fire.

J.R. and I were in the same Old Testament Survey class. During one class, our professor showed us a video of Harold Kushner speaking about his book *When Bad Things Happen to Good People*.

When I'd lived in Indiana as a preteen, I'd heard about God's plan from the people in our first church. God had everything all mapped out. "There's a reason for everything," they'd told me. But Kushner challenged that. He said suffering *wasn't* part of the plan, God *didn't* cause it, and you couldn't avoid it just by doing all the "correct" things.

He talked about how, instead of blaming the predator, we blame a woman for the way she dresses when she's assaulted. Like she brought it on herself. I didn't hear what he said for a while after that because all I could hear was Jackie in my ear. *Can you blame him with the way you dress?*

Maybe Ray was always going to do this, no matter how perfect of a Christian or a person I might have been. Maybe it didn't matter that I'd slept with Ben or wore shorts or forgot to pray. Harold Kushner never met me, but he was the first person to say it out loud to me. *It's not your fault.*

After the video, I didn't feel like going to my next class. J.R. skipped his next class too, and we walked around campus, not really heading anywhere at all. "Do you think I'm 'good people?'" I asked him.

He raised an eyebrow at me. "Nobody's good."

Act Normal

I was over at DeRoy's with Mom and Dad when Angela burst through the back door, all in a huff, and said, "Well, now you've got a dropout for a daughter. What do you think about that?"

Her credits were screwed up from the transfer from Arkansas. The school had let her enroll and took my parents' tuition money without mentioning they had different graduation requirements from our high school in Arkansas. The principal sat her down and told her she was short on credits and wouldn't get to graduate in May, but she could always come back and finish up next year.

The way she told it, she threw a book, told him to shove his diploma up his ass, grabbed her backpack, and stomped off campus while he yelled after her that she couldn't leave on her own because she was a minor.

Maybe part of her wanted my parents to blow up, but they were too defeated by that point to care much. If she wanted to drop out and get her GED, she could.

When I told J.R. I wanted to do something to cheer her up, he drove Angela and me to the movie theater, paid for our tickets, and bought us each a large pop.

Dad went over to Pastor Dave's house and brought Angela's stuff back to the pink-flowered room at DeRoy's. He drove her down to a testing center so she could get her GED, and after that, she got a full-time job at a shoe store, which made her the only person in the family with a full-time job. Dad was still searching for a church, but Mennonite congregations choose their own pastors, and search committees move slowly.

CHAPTER TWENTY-EIGHT

Six months after running away to Indiana, I sat on the floor of an empty classroom with a dozen women and listened to a large, loud man tell us to "always go for the balls."

I thought it was weird for a pacifist college to offer a free women's self-defense class, but when I saw the flier, I got excited. On the night of the class, I pulled my long hair back into the most severe high ponytail I could manage and strode across campus like the kind of badass I suspected I really was inside.

We spent the first half of the class hearing about all the precautionary measures we ought to take to avoid getting raped. Always be aware of your surroundings. Park in well-lit areas. Check the back seat before getting into your car. And if someone still manages to grab you, scream, "Fire!" instead of rape because people actually care if there's a fire. It didn't make me feel all that empowered to know that people would trip all over themselves to help if a fire started up, but nobody would bother to turn their heads if I was *just* being raped.

Each of us took turns learning how to escape different holds and how to trip our attacker and throw him off balance so we could run away. I got chastised a little because I forgot to go for the balls, but in my defense, ball punching was a new sport for me.

I was proud of myself for going. Even though I got a little irritated that I was expected to constantly be on my guard, learning how to physically resist an attack made me feel like less of a victim. If Ray ever showed up, at least I'd have a few solid ideas about how to get away. Anyway, shouting, "Fire!" if Ray was near probably wouldn't even be a lie.

Besides, I didn't see much point in being a pacifist by default. Is it really pacifism if you *can't* defend yourself? I didn't think so. Real, honest, Jesus-like pacifism was being able to defend yourself, but *choosing* a different path, for the sake of the gospel. It had to be a choice to count. It had to be Dirk Willems turning back when he could have kept running.

Life was starting to feel more settled. I still missed my friends and my old life, but I didn't feel as homesick as I had in the beginning. Warmer spring days got me out of my dorm room more often, and I started taking long walks around campus.

One afternoon, I was hungry earlier than usual, so I went down to the cafeteria without J.R. While I was balancing my tray and searching for an empty seat, a petite girl with short blonde hair walked up and asked, "Are you Kristy?"

I couldn't place her at first, but when she mentioned Mr. Gerber's class, a little girl with long blonde hair popped into my head. Her name was Emily. We'd gone to fifth grade together, just after my family had moved from Texas to Indiana.

We hadn't known each other well. I'd only gone to that school for a year, and we hadn't been close. I couldn't understand how she remembered me at all, but she even remembered I'd moved there from Texas. She said she recognized me right away because I looked exactly the same, which made me cringe a little since I'd mostly run around in outdated Goodwill dresses, neon stretch pants, and red ropers back then.

She seemed genuinely happy to run into me, which threw me for a loop after months of walking into the cafeteria without so much as a "hey there" from most of the other students. Even though I'd chickened out on contacting my old friends, it was exciting to run into someone who'd known me *before*. I'd been so hung up on clinging to my roots in Arkansas, I'd forgotten I had some roots in Indiana too.

We talked a little about where we'd been and what we'd done over the past eight years. It was the first real conversation I'd had with anyone other than J.R. or my down-the-hall Spanish soap-loving neighbor. It was just a lunchtime chat between old acquaintances, but it was such a relief. Every time my family moved, I assumed everyone forgot about me as soon as the U-Haul pulled out. They had their own lives to live, and I was just a quick little blip who never stuck around long.

I figured everyone in Arkansas had already forgotten about me. Ben would've moved on to a new girlfriend. My friends would be hanging out with other people. Sunday church services would grind on without my presence, just like they had while I was marooned in Conway. My absence wouldn't change anyone's life, so why would they ever spare me a thought?

But Emily from fifth grade remembered me after eight years. And if Emily remembered me, maybe I didn't just fade away for the people I left behind. Maybe they thought about me sometimes. Maybe they missed me. I'd been grieving the loss of people I loved, but it'd never occurred to me that they lost me too.

CHAPTER TWENTY-NINE

J.R. and I sat side by side on the common room couch, watching a movie, like we did almost every night. By the time the movie ended, my head was propped up on the armrest, and I was about ready to fall asleep right there so I wouldn't have to walk all the way down the hall to my room.

J.R. leaned over me and started chatting away, but I wasn't paying attention. Maybe he asked what movie we should watch the next day. Or he complained about a class or made a joke.

His voice droned on for a while, and as my eyes started to close, he reached out and picked up my right hand. He held it for a second, palm up like he was reading the lines. Then he turned my hand over, cupped his hand around mine, bent my elbow, and lowered my hand back down to my left breast.

Most people say when you panic, your fight-or-flight instinct kicks in. Either you fight off the threat or you try to get away from it as fast as you can. But that's not always true. Sometimes you freeze instead.

Adrenaline pumped through me, and I wasn't tired at all anymore, but I didn't move. I didn't fling his hand off and sock him in the mouth. I didn't hightail it off the couch and to the safety of my room. I didn't use any of my fancy new self-defense moves or punch him in the balls.

I just lay there and tapped into my go-to coping mechanism—denial.

Stop overreacting. He was making a point about heartbeats or something, and that's why he moved my hand. If I'd been paying attention to whatever it was he was talking about, I'd know what this was all about. So, really, it was my fault for being a bad friend and not listening.

He smiled down at me, but I don't know what he could have read in my owl-eyed face to warrant a smile. I suppose he interpreted my silence as consent because he squeezed my hand—hard—which squeezed my breast. Hard. Pain snapped me back to life. He made me hurt myself, and that was what qualified as over-the-line for me. "What're you doing?"

He laughed. "Living vicariously through your hand."

I didn't know why he thought it was acceptable. I'd never even flirted with him. I'd never done anything to make him think I'd welcome that sort of contact.

"Well, stop," I said, knowing he might not and I couldn't remember a single thing from my self-defense class except that I was supposed to scream about fire.

His hand lingered over mine for a few more breaths before he drew it off, tracing his fingers down my arm as he went.

I was off the couch and halfway to the door when he asked, "Where you going?"

"Bed." He smiled at that too.

Back in my room, I lay awake all night. It felt like a violation, but when I compared J.R. to Ray, it didn't seem like that big of a deal. What J.R. had done was wrong, but what Ray had done was worse, wasn't it? When you're fighting the big battles, don't you have to let the little ones go sometimes? Was being groped by a boy I'd trusted a *little* battle?

I didn't want to see J.R. again, but was that fair? It didn't occur to me that friendship wasn't a right, and I didn't have to spend time with anyone I didn't want to spend time with.

The next day, I called Dad. He was quiet while the previous night ricocheted around my head and out my mouth. At the end, I asked, "Is it OK to be upset?"

Because I honestly didn't know. He didn't rape me. Or kill me. Or *threaten* to kill me. And that had to count for something.

Maybe all boys did stuff like that and I'd just been sheltered from it because, other than that one time with Matt, I'd mostly been around Ben, who I didn't mind grabbing me, or Daniel, who was basically my brother.

"Of course it's OK to be upset!" Dad yelled.

He went on about boys and respect, and I put a hand over the speaker so he wouldn't hear me crying on the other end. I moved my hand away now and then, to give a watery "uh-huh."

At first I was relieved to have permission to feel betrayed and angry, but right behind relief was shame because I should have known that I had a right to feel any damn way I felt. But my experiences with Ray and our church had me turned so upside down that I couldn't seem to trust my own reactions. I had a hard time understanding the only person who had a right to me was me.

Dad wound down, and I pulled myself together long enough to tell him I'd confront J.R. and tell him we couldn't be friends anymore. Dad wanted me to get our resident adviser involved, but I didn't want to make a big deal about it. J.R. was usually a nice guy, and it was just the one time, and he had stopped—eventually—when I told him to. I'd just end our friendship and be done with it. "I'll deal with it myself," I said.

J.R. stopped by my room a little while later. I stood in my doorway and told him I didn't want to hang out with him anymore, but he didn't understand what my problem was. "You groped me," I said.

He leaned against the doorframe and said I misunderstood the situation, but I couldn't think of any innocent reason why he'd need to make me grab my own breast.

I crossed my arms in front of my chest. "I don't want to be your girlfriend."

"Yeah, I know that."

"Then why grab me like that?"

"I didn't." He even managed to keep a straight face.

"We can't be friends anymore."

He wanted to know why, like I hadn't just told him why.

I was tired of playing his game. "You know why, but whatever. I don't *need* a reason why."

I skipped classes and every meal that day so I

wouldn't run into him.

The next morning, he came to my dorm room again. He wanted to talk it out. I told him to go away.

The day after that, he came back as I was leaving for class. He followed me all the way across the train tracks and across campus. When I left class, he was waiting outside the building. He didn't try to talk to me, but just watched me as I walked back toward my dorm.

Dad said I had to speak to our RA, so I sat down with Gabby in her apartment and filled her in. She agreed J.R. was out of line and assured me she'd talk to him. He didn't come by my room that day at all, but the day after, he left a note on my door saying he wanted to talk. I marched over to Gabby's and asked if she'd spoken to him yet. She had. I showed her the note, and she promised to talk to him again.

I stopped attending the Old Testament class I shared with J.R. and adjusted my eating schedule to avoid him in the cafeteria. The Bible study group wasn't an option for me anymore, so I was cut off from the only group of Christians I had any real connection to. Again.

Nightmares hit me full force. The girls in my hall started to tease me about being a vampire because I slept during the day and roamed the halls at night. While roaming around after midnight, I ripped into myself because there had to be some reason this kept happening to me, some reason why my only friend was doing this. I was doing something wrong, and if I didn't figure out how I was causing this to happen, I'd never have control of my life.

CHAPTER THIRTY

I started keeping a daily log. It wasn't a log of all the times J.R. followed me or tried to make contact, which it should have been. Instead, I started logging what I wore each day and made a note of every interaction I had with male students.

On the day the shaggy-haired boy from the floor-sitting Mennonite church parked at my table, I was wearing shorts. He made a joke about the spring weather being too cold for my shorts, and I made a joke about it being too cold for his sandals.

When I wore my black tank top, two boys asked to sit at my table, and I thought I might be onto something until they ignored me to continue whatever conversation they'd been in the middle of before sitting down.

I had to figure out if I was doing something to signal men like Ray and J.R. There had to be some reason men like that gravitated toward me. If I could gather enough data, I'd know what it was. Thanks to Jackie, my first hypothesis was that my haphazard way of dressing was some sort of irresistible siren call for easily obsessed men. If all I had to do was dress differently, that was an easy fix. However, I hadn't noticed any trend in the data I'd collected so far. What I wore or how I fixed my hair or how heavy my makeup was didn't seem to change the amount or type of attention I got.

Still, it couldn't be a coincidence that I'd run away from one stalker and straight into another. Even though I didn't readily admit it, that's what J.R. was. When a girl tells you to stay away, and you don't, and she's forced to adjust her schedule to avoid you, and you force her to pay attention to you by following her around and leaving notes, it's not romantic. It's criminal.

Angela called me one afternoon. J.R. showed up at the shoe store where she worked and hung around, asking questions about me. She couldn't get him to leave for a long time, and it scared her. My sister, who'd been ripped out of her home during her senior year of high school, who'd given up her prom and her class trip and even her graduation ceremony, who'd lost her boyfriend when we fled to Indiana, had to deal with yet another one of my creepy guys who wouldn't take "no" for an answer.

I was scared too. Ray started out by leaving little notes, if you considered magazine and Bible pages notes. I knew where little notes could lead. I told J.R. to stop. Gabby told him to stop. He didn't listen. Just like Ray. When he got tired of me telling him to go away, was he going to want revenge? Was I going to start getting scratched out brides shoved under my dorm room door?

At dinner that night, nobody sat with me in the cafeteria, so I made a note in the composition book and went to put my tray away. A girl from J.R.'s Bible study group was putting her tray away too, and she asked where I'd been. I knew how well it went over when you told Christians someone was stalking you, so I told her "something" happened with J.R. and I wasn't comfortable attending anymore.

She probably assumed we were dating and broke up, which was fine by me because it didn't require a lot of explanation. We stood by the tray return, chatting for a little while. I was about to ask for her phone number, so we could hang out sometime, when J.R. walked up with a friendly "hi" to me, like we were best buddies.

He thought he could get away with it because of our audience. I'd have to play nice and act like everything was fine. No way would I make some huge, embarrassing scene in front of all the students in the cafeteria.

My hands flew to my hips and I planted my feet. "You're supposed to stay away from me."

The Bible study girl looked confused, and J.R. had the gall to mirror her expression, like this was the first he'd heard of it. "Why?" he asked.

My voice rose. "You know exactly why, you pervert."

"I don't know what I did." He stayed calm and cool in front of everyone, like that sort of man does. Because who would believe an emotional young woman over a calm and composed man?

I snapped. "Look," I shouted, causing the girl and J.R. to flinch and the nearby tables to quiet down to see what the fuss was about, "I don't need another stalker. Leave me alone. And if you *ever* go near my sister again, I'll kill you."

His eyes widened, and I was shaking so hard by that

Act Normal

point, trying to repress the urge to jump at him right then, I think he even believed me. I sure believed me when I slowly ground out that last sentence again, just so he and I would be clear. "I swear to God, *I will kill you*."

I whipped around before he could reply and strode out of the cafeteria, still shaking with all the rage I felt toward both of the men who'd manipulated my life just because they could. I expected him to follow me, but he didn't.

Minutes later, I stood in the middle of my too-bright hallway and stared at the plastic Wal-Mart bag hanging off my doorknob. The bag was weighed down with something bulky.

Even though I didn't want to touch it, I pulled it off the door and entered my room. I had to look, and putting it off wasn't going to change what was in there.

My backpack dropped off my shoulders and thumped onto my bed. I took a deep breath, reminded myself I could handle anything inside the bag, and yanked it open so hard one of the handles snapped.

A teddy bear smiled up at me. He held a red plush heart. I wanted to rip his grizzly little head off. My hands shook as I wrapped the bear back up in the plastic bag and set the crinkling mess on my desk.

I reflected back on the threat I'd made in the cafeteria, right in front of all those pacifist students. For the second time that year, I had to ask myself a hard question. If it came down to it, would I take someone's life? It's not a question most North American pacifists face. At least it's not a question most *male* pacifists face.

They can play theoretical games about home invasions and government drafts that'll never happen. For women, it isn't just a theoretical question. It's never a case of *if* a man tries to hurt us, but *when*. What will we do *when* it happens?

After Dad heard about the bear and J.R.'s visit to Angela, he set up a meeting with the dean of students. Dad and I sat at a round table in a bare conference room and explained the situation. The dean thought J.R. just had a crush on me. What was the harm in that? But Dad made it clear that we knew exactly what stalking was and filled him in on our recent past.

"We're not doing this again," Dad said. "My daughter's afraid to be on your campus. Either you take care of it or I will." And even though Dad was supposed to be a man of peace, he was still a tall guy with a booming voice, and the dean took him seriously and promised to handle it.

Angela and I ran into J.R. and his friend at Wal-Mart a few days later. They spotted us, and J.R. held eye contact with me and walked straight at us. When Angela moved to walk down a side aisle to avoid him, I said, "uh-uh" and played chicken with him, Angela walking a half-step behind me. *He* should move, not me. I wasn't the one who had done anything wrong. His friend forcefully grabbed J.R. by the arm and propelled him down a side aisle.

That was the last I saw of J.R. He never left another note or stuffed animal, but it was too late. I was flunking all my classes by then, so I dropped out and moved back into DeRoy's.

I wonder if J.R. graduated on time. I bet he did.

The first person I'd opened up to about Ray had picked up right where Ray left off. For a long time, I figured J.R. saw me as an easy target. He planned to get close, earn my trust, and then take what he wanted.

But now I don't think he saw it that way. I don't think he saw what he was doing as stalking. He just didn't think my rights were as important as his. It was a free campus, after all. He had just as much of a right to be in my dorm hall as anyone else, didn't he? He felt like he had the right to walk through campus right behind me and impose his presence on me and steal my attention, even when I didn't want to give it. He had the right to speak to me and force me to hear him, even when I didn't want to listen. And who was I to deny him any of that? Just some girl.

It was easy to blame Ray's actions on his mental illness, but that obviously wasn't the whole problem. J.R. didn't have a mental illness. He'd never experienced delusions. He was just an average guy. Unremarkable, in every way.

Ray's delusions contributed to his obsession with me, and they made the situation more dangerous, but they hadn't *caused* him to start stalking me. Plenty of people are diagnosed with schizophrenia and never hurt anyone. What did Ray and J.R. have in common, then? Possibly, the way they read scripture.

How much did J.R.'s rejection of reading scripture in context influence him? Did he take those passages about women being submissive and apply them to all women, in all times, in all situations? Did he apply them to me? Did he expect me to submit to him, no matter what he wanted, just because I was a woman and he was a man? Was that what Ray had done?

I don't know how J.R. justified his actions, but he did justify them and somehow square what he was doing to me with his faith. They had both managed to do that.

CHAPTER THIRTY-ONE

Dad held his glasses in one hand and cried into the other. I'd seen him cry a few times before, but not like that.

He sat on DeRoy's couch next to me, his two-time college dropout daughter, and lowered his hand to stare across the room at Angela, his high school dropout daughter.

Angela looked like she wanted to chuck something at his head. "I don't care," she said.

He wiped his eyes and blinked, before telling the floor, "I can't even get my daughter to her prom."

Richard Simmons had a TV show called *Dream Makers*. People wrote in and asked for help to make their dreams come true. Dad, who was still optimistic in ways that baffled the rest of us, wrote to the show, explaining our situation and asking for help to pay for transportation so Angela could attend what would have been her senior prom. If he could pull it off, if Angela could have this one normal thing, then maybe she'd be OK. He never heard back from the show, and he took it as a personal failure. He still didn't have a church. Or an income. Or a home.

"I mean it," Angela said, "I don't even want to go.

I hate Pine Creek."

I wasn't sure how honest she was being, but I kept my mouth shut. I went to my prom with Ben and all the kids I'd gone to school with since the ninth grade. I didn't have the right to an opinion.

Dad wiped his face again and put his glasses back on. "I'm sorry," he told her. "You deserve to go."

Angela jerked her shoulders into a shrug and rolled her eyes. "Yeah, well, whoever said life's fair?"

Those were the same words Dad used to say to us when we'd complain about not getting a candy bar or a Coke at the store. It was his job, as a parent, to teach us we couldn't always get what we wanted, even if we didn't think it was fair. Maybe if he'd known how things would go, he'd have just bought us the candy.

In May, I was hired for a job I wasn't qualified for: administrative assistant for the customer service department of a major RV manufacturer. Everyone in the department was a woman, even my supervisor, who also supervised all the men who worked in the warehouse. I was only nineteen, but my boss wanted someone she could teach from scratch, who wouldn't have any bad habits picked up from other jobs. I could type fast and I was *completely* inexperienced, so the job was mine.

My boss was the most interesting woman I'd ever met. She yelled at men, and they *let her*. It was the first time I'd ever seen a woman who was in charge. I was fascinated. The woman who trained me said my boss had a temper. She threw stuff around her office sometimes when warehouse orders got really screwed up, but she was nice to me and said I was the only person in the whole company who could walk into her office without knocking first. It sounds stupid, but that made me feel important, and I hadn't felt important in a while.

Angela and I drove to Goodwill so I could buy outdated skirt suits that didn't fit. I camouflaged the scuff marks on my white pumps with Wite-Out and painted clear nail polish down the runs in my pantyhose every morning and hoped nobody noticed. When I got my first paycheck, I pranced into JCPenney and bought a pink skirt suit and *three* pairs of pantyhose.

All the women in the office seemed to like me. I was quiet, but I was a fast worker. And when the fax toner exploded, I laughed it off and cleaned it up instead of swearing up a storm, so they said I had a great attitude.

Two months into my job, a Mennonite church from a small town in northern Michigan contacted Dad.

Comins, Michigan: Population 420. It was a one-bar town you could pitch a baseball across. The nearest Wal-Mart was an hour away and so was the nearest community college. It used to be the end of the train line, when there *was* a train.

In July 1999, a tornado had taken out most of the town. The post office, church, and parsonage were wiped out. At the same time I'd been in Oklahoma, working with a Mennonite Disaster Service crew to rebuild tornado-damaged houses (while Ray was breaking into *my* house), another MDS crew had been in Comins, working to rebuild the church and parsonage.

My family drove six hours north to visit the church. The church building was new, and the people were friendly and asked me things like, "Are you in college?" because they didn't understand what a difficult question that was for me to answer. I told them, "I'm taking some time off to work and save money," because it wasn't exactly a lie, and it sounded like something a responsible, respectable pastor's daughter might do.

Dad needed a church, and this seemed like a good one, so I spent most of the visit keeping my dang mouth shut so I wouldn't slip up and reveal myself to be the wayward daughter I was. Because who would hire a pastor with a daughter like *me*?

Nobody told me that Mom and Dad had already told the pastoral search committee about our trouble in Arkansas, so I sat in my pink suit with Wite-Out pumps and pretended to be the most normal person they'd ever met. I knew all the correct answers. "I was always very involved in the youth group." "Yes, I'd love to go to the movies with the other kids sometime." "This is the kind of church I could really see us in."

While I passed out those carefully coiffed comments, I already knew there was no way I could be what I'd been. Those people probably would have loved me a couple of years ago. I'd have swept through there, going on about outreach and service projects and being all-around hyper for the Holy Ghost. But my statements were controlled now, and measured to belt out just enough God-ishness to prove I wasn't a total heathen, while not committing myself to actually being involved if they hired Dad. Maybe I could survive slipping in at the last second on Sunday mornings and sitting in the back so I could make a quick exit when service was over. But that would be it. I wouldn't be leading any Bible studies or writing any skits or worrying about outreach. That fire was long gone.

When the church decided to hire Dad, I had to make a choice. Technically, I didn't have to go. I had a good job in Indiana, and one of my coworkers offered to let me stay with her for a few months until I could find an apartment.

I told Dad I wasn't sure what I should do. What if I made the wrong choice?

He said most decisions in life aren't about right or wrong. There are a lot of right paths. The most important thing is not to get stuck. Pick a path, and if it ends up not being the path you belong on, then pick a new path. Just keep moving forward.

I gave my notice at work and told my awesome boss that I'd decided to go back to school and would be living with my parents in Michigan to save money while I did that. Really, though, I didn't care about school. I just didn't want to be alone.

Part Three

AUGUST 2000
COMINS, MICHIGAN

How long, LORD? Will you forget me forever?
How long will you hide your face from me?
How long must I wrestle with my thoughts
and day after day have sorrow in my heart?
How long will my enemy triumph over me?

—Psalm 13:1-2

CHAPTER THIRTY-TWO

I stretched out in the truck bed, hovering somewhere between bored and buzzed. Elle, the extroverted brunette I'd met a few days ago, was off in the woods with some guy. I hadn't anticipated the rapid temperature drop, so I was only wearing my gray pleather jacket. It wasn't enough for a late August night in northern Michigan.

Another day, Elle and her mother would ferry me to a warehouse store to stock up on genuine Up North clothes. They'd steer me through rows of Carhartt coveralls and toward the discount hoodies and gloves and hats and, "No, I can't imagine I'd ever need snow pants."

For now, I was freezing my bony ass off. I passed a bottle of Schnapps around with her forest friend's brother, who kept bragging about his Britney Spears sunglasses, and a couple of other boys I didn't know.

They teased me for lighting a new cigarette with the end of my old one. One of them called me a chain-smoker. I didn't care. The repetitive motions always kept me calm. Inhale, withdraw, exhale, flick.

I dozed off—or passed out—and woke up to someone moving near me. I kept my eyes squeezed tight and started up a mental mantra of, "Stupid! Stupid! Stupid!" because I knew better than to fall asleep around a bunch of drunk guys I didn't even know. Hell, I knew better than to fall asleep around a close friend.

A coat fell over me, and one of the boys moved back to his end of the truck bed. "What?" he asked whoever was snickering. "She's shaking."

I stayed there under the coat that smelled like a stranger and pretended to sleep until Elle got back. It'd been ten months since I was last hugged. Four months since I was last groped by a friend. And some random boy in the woods, who probably didn't even catch my name, just gave me the coat off his back.

Elle and I ran into the boys a few days later on campus at the community college we attended. I prodded a little and tried to find out who had covered me up, but nobody owned up to it. Whoever it was had earned a loyal friend in me, though. That was all it took to earn my loyalty. I'd set the bar about as low as it could go. Just don't assault me and we'll be BFFs for life.

I was thankful for Elle. She was persistent enough to get me out of the house, and she seemed to know everyone, which made meeting people easier for me. All I had to do was tag along with her. Mostly, I stuck with her and Angela, who was starting her freshman year on campus with me.

We had to drive an hour to get to a community college that stood in the middle of nowhere. It was surrounded by Kirtland's warbler habitat, which was also the school's mascot. Those birds only live in new growth forests, which means fire is a warbler's best friend. It burns down the old trees to make room for new growth. It was a little on the nose.

Dad was preaching in a brand-new church building, and we were living in a brand-new house, with brand-new textured carpet. It was the nicest place we'd ever lived, which made me terrified of doing something to screw it up for us.

At first I put out some effort and attended church on Sunday mornings. That was what people expected the pastor's daughter to do. Dad suggested I join a Sunday school class that was starting up. Most of the people in it were adult children of alcoholics, but it was supposed to be for anyone who'd had a hard time.

I sat through one class. When it was my turn to speak, I didn't talk about Ray, because there was no way I could explain that, so instead I ranted about how much pressure I was under to be perfect and never show any emotion, which was mostly pressure I'd put on myself.

Arkansas was my fault. If I'd been a better person, if I hadn't made that stupid website, if I hadn't fooled around with Ben, if I hadn't gotten up behind the pulpit and gone all fire and brimstone, nobody would have sided with Ray. I'd made it too easy for them to choose him.

Emotions scared me now. I'd survived for almost a year with any unproductive emotion stomped down. Anger was a productive emotion. Anger got shit done. But grief? Grief was useless. I didn't let myself grieve because I was afraid once I got going with it, I'd never stop, and I had a life to live here. But when I numbed down grief, I numbed down joy with it, so I lived in a steady limbo where I wasn't exactly happy and I wasn't exactly sad, and the only feelings that seeped through the cracks were anxiety and anger, which were both fear when you got right down to it. But it always flew out of my mouth as rage.

The middle-aged adults in class all seemed so surprised by my hostile tone that I couldn't stomach going back. I didn't want people to look at me like that. Like they didn't quite know what to make of me or do with me. Like I was too damaged for the damaged-people class.

When I started working as a drugstore cashier a couple of towns over, I took any Sunday morning shift I could get. It was a handy excuse to keep me out of church. People understood if you had to work. They wouldn't understand if I just couldn't stand to go.

It took me a month to start unpacking my stuff. A month before I started to think we might be able to stay. I sat on the floor of my new bedroom, right next to a window with brand-new locks that *stayed* locked, and unpacked boxes that had been in DeRoy's barn for almost a year.

Mom and Dad bought me a new computer desk and matching bookshelf. I'd never had brand-new furniture before. Everything I'd ever owned came from garage sales or auctions. Mom called the new furniture "birthday presents," but they gave them to me in August and my birthday had been back in March.

I stacked *Mesopotamian Myths* next to my collection of Jack Handey books. Porcelain dolls and the participation trophy I got for playing basketball in the first grade went up on the long shelf above my desk. I pulled a Ken doll that was dressed like a groom out of the box. He used to stand on my shelf next to a Barbie bride, but she'd been burned up. Ken went back into the box.

The CDs came out next. Tom Petty and the Heartbreakers. Then Audio Adrenaline, Jars of Clay, DC Talk, and the Newsboys.

The Newsboys CD popped right out of its jewel case. In eleventh grade, I'd listened to "Shine" on repeat for months. The song said if you shined strong enough, even someone with schizophrenia would come around. I guess I hadn't shone brightly enough. I cracked the disc down the middle, and it split into two unequal pieces. It felt so good, the rest of my Christian music collection followed before I tossed all the jagged pieces into the black garbage bag at the foot of my bed.

Dad kept insisting I was angry at God, and maybe I was a little. I'd prayed the day we left Arkansas. I stood in the sanctuary, in front of the altar, and prayed—hard—for a last-minute miracle. For Travis to come running through the double doors and announce Ray had turned himself in and admitted to everything, so we could go ahead and unload the moving truck. It could happen. If I had faith as big as a mustard seed, it could happen. *Shine*, and it could happen.

But I didn't get a miracle. I got an eleven-hour drive to Indiana, trying to keep up with Dad, who was ahead of me in a U-Haul truck, while Angela sat beside me in our van, screaming that I was driving like a maniac and was going to kill us. Then I got J.R. Either God hadn't heard my prayer, or he didn't care.

Maybe if I'd paid closer attention, I'd have noticed I also got away with my life and the lives of my family. And I got DeRoy's generosity, and lunch with Emily from fifth grade, and kids from Pine Creek who offered to help me when nobody else would.

Mostly, I was ashamed. I'd been blind to what those church council members really were. I'd let them trick me into believing I belonged there with them. That they loved me. I thought they were good Christians, but they sure didn't act much like people who'd ever read anything Jesus said. I should have seen that. I should have known not to trust them.

I'd learned not to trust them now, though, which opened its own can of worms. Most of my religious education had taken place in that church, and if I couldn't trust the people who'd taught me, could I trust any of the lessons I'd learned there? They were wrong about Ray. They were wrong about courtship. They were probably wrong about a lot of things.

In Goshen, I'd run across people who believed in God *and* evolution. They said you could be a Christian and believe humans evolved from an early mammal, but I didn't see how you could. If you didn't believe God created humans, as is, then you didn't believe the Bible. If you didn't believe the Bible, how could you be a Christian? Creationism didn't make sense to me, but if I couldn't be a Christian without believing God had created the world in exactly six days, then I wouldn't call myself a Christian anymore.

Maybe my old church was even wrong about God. Those people said God was real, but what did they know?

All I knew was fundamentalism and when that thread started unraveling, everything unraveled. I said I wasn't a Christian. I was a Christ-follower because, even if I couldn't wrap my head around Genesis, I at least still liked Jesus. But soon I dropped even that label, and then I was nothing at all.

CHAPTER THIRTY-THREE

The silver sedan followed Angela's blue Tempo from Comins to Fairview, then pulled up to the gas pump alongside us. A boy about our age got out, flashed us a smile like he knew us, and grabbed the pump.

A few hours later, Angela and I were walking around campus between classes when I spotted the same boy walking out of the Student Center. I tapped Angela's arm. "Isn't that the guy from this morning?"

Gas station boy grinned at us from several yards away, and we returned his friendly greeting with down-turned eyebrows. "Is he following us?" Angela asked.

We stared at him hard, but he went right on smiling like we were the friendliest damn people he'd ever run across. I cupped one hand around my mouth and yelled across the distance, "Hey! Who the hell are you?"

His smile widened even more as he walked on over to us as if I hadn't been the least bit hostile and said, "Hi, I'm David."

He told us he'd just moved to Comins from downstate. He held up his left hand, like all good Michiganders do, and pointed to the lower right section of his palm. He'd spotted us around Comins a few times.

Act Normal

Knowing how small the population of Comins was, I figured it wasn't very likely we'd meet many other people our age who lived so close, so I gave him our phone number. He said he'd give us a call and we could all hang out sometime.

As soon as he walked off, Angela lit into me. What was I thinking, giving our number out to a total stranger like that?

"Not everyone we meet's a stalker, Angela."

"Everyone *you* meet's a stalker."

Luckily, David wasn't a stalker, and the three of us started hanging out. He was a name-brand clothes kind of kid, with the sort of up-for-anything, charismatic personality that made everyone like him.

We wasted hours playing pool and Ping-Pong in the Student Center, which was a lot more fun than attending classes. And if I was bored at 9:00 on a Wednesday night, all I had to do was call David up and we'd drive over to Alpena for no reason at all. His answer to, "Do you wanna . . . ?" was always, "Yes."

Angela buckled down and got on top of her schoolwork, but I was making up for lost time. I'd lost a year of my life dealing with Ray and J.R., and even before that, I'd wasted four years being Miss Morality to impress a church and a God that didn't give a rat's ass about me being murdered.

Hanging around the theater department was a safe way of enjoying the presence of other humans without having to "open up" or "get real." I auditioned for a role in *Crimes of the Heart*, and I was cast because of my authentic southern accent. The director asked me to act as "accent coach" for the other actors, but the only advice I gave them was to say "pee-can" instead of "pee-cahn" because that's how we said it down south. We didn't really, but it was fun to make those Yankees say "pee-can" in front of an audience.

Before rehearsal one night, a goateed actor picked me up, carried me across the stage, and sat down on a set chair with me on the edge of his knees. "Ho, ho, ho! And what do you want for Christmas, little girl?"

I asked Santa for a fifth of vodka in my stocking.

"Only if you're a very good girl," he said, and gave me a pat on the head with his left hand while wrapping his other arm around my waist so I wouldn't fall backward off his lap.

It was the first time anyone had touched me in the past year. At least it was the first touch that wasn't the kind of bad touch McGruff the Crime Dog had warned me about in third grade.

This other actor had a girlfriend, who was standing off to the side of the stage, laughing at us. He wasn't attracted to me. I wasn't interested in him like that either, but I didn't want to get up.

I reached out with both hands and framed his face to make him look at me. "Santa. Listen. This is extremely important . . . " and I listed off naughty things the rest of the cast had supposedly done. It played off as a bit, but really, it was just an excuse to sit there a little longer with someone's arm around me.

One year after my last real hug, and three years after

signing a virginity pledge, I showed up at Gary's door with a plastic candy cane full of tiny flavored vodka samples one of my older coworkers had bought for me. I knew him a little through Elle. He was about the most laid back boy I knew, and I knew he'd be easy. I mean, it's not exactly hard to seduce a college-aged boy.

A boy from my algebra class was next. I figured it wasn't wrong because I also developed a strict code of conduct.

Don't have sex with your friends.
Don't have sex with a boy who has a girlfriend.
Don't have sex with boys your friends are into.
Don't have sex with anyone you actually like (because, hey, I didn't want to hurt anyone I liked).

People may have thought I was a slut, but I was an ethical slut, dammit.

One-night stands satisfied my need for physical human contact and gave me a sense of control. Part of me figured if I was going to be objectified anyway, I might as well be the one calling the shots. Besides, boys took advantage of girls all the time, so I figured it was only fair if I did the same thing to them. It was either use them or risk them using me, and I'd much rather be a whore than a victim.

As long as I kept up my pseudo-feminist mantra of "I don't do blow jobs," (because why should they get something when I wasn't getting anything in return?), I claimed each one-night stand as a victory for women, while conveniently forgetting I always got drunk first.

Almost every week, David invited Angela and me to go bowling with his friends, but that sounded boring, so I always sent Angela off on her own. Through David she got to know other local boys while I mostly hung around Elle and guys I disliked enough to have sex with.

The only person who managed to crack my shell a little was David, and that was mainly because he ignored half of what I did or said. He and I usually didn't talk about much of anything really, other than one night when we sat around with Elle in her basement, telling secrets to one another, and I admitted to being engaged once, which surprised the hell out of them.

Other than that, I didn't mention my past. There was no point. And how do you even approach that sort of an introduction? "Hi, my name's Kristy. Let me tell you about the time a friend of the family tried to set me on fire for being a whore."

I didn't want to be the girl who'd almost been murdered. I wanted a boring, normal backstory. When people asked why I'd moved to Michigan, I wanted to be able to say, "Because my dad's a pastor and a church up here hired him," without feeling guilty about leaving out the most important part of that story.

One night, Elle's mom sat all the girls down and lectured us about not falling in love too young. Elle told her not to bother telling me because I *never* fell in love. I never even fell in like.

That's how they saw me. Detached. And I was. It was safer for me that way. I was always around other people without actually being *with* other people. We could have a good time, but if they rejected me for any reason, I could tell myself they hadn't really rejected *me* because they didn't know me well enough to reject me.

Living life without any attachments takes a toll, though. When you're just going through the motions, it's hard to set any sort of goals. I couldn't bring myself to care about school, and my grades slipped, so the people around me knew two concrete facts: I liked to have one-nights stands, and I was too stupid for community college. That drove Angela straight up the wall.

She walked into the game room one afternoon and slammed herself into a chair at my table. The other day, she'd overheard a couple of guys from the theater department making fun of me. "They said you're dumb," she said, all full of indignation on my behalf.

"Why do I care?" I asked, and went on sopping up pizza grease with my napkin.

She'd cared enough to bring my ACT scores in so she could shove them into their faces and tell those guys that her sister was a genius.

I shot a sideways glance at the kids playing pool. "Ang, I'm not a genius." (For the record, I'm not.)

But she needed me to be smart. Because that's how it'd always been. That was our normal. If I wasn't the book-smart, introverted, Bible-thumping sister, then what was I?

Angela was almost always around to yank me back

when I started going too far off the rails, and that pissed me off. I didn't want anyone to think I was smart. I didn't want people to have high expectations of me.

Maybe Angela told David some nice things about me. If she didn't, then I don't know what he was thinking bringing his roommate, Andy, over to my house to meet me. I got home from work after everyone else was there and found Elle talking to a boy who was a head and a half taller than I was and very, very quiet.

I don't remember what I said when I walked into the room, but I know it was something weird that I thought was funny. I was always doing that. One time, I walked into Elle's house and tried to get everyone to come with me to find a beaver I was sure I'd just hit with my car. I promised to make a hat out of it and everyone would get a turn wearing it. Nobody would go with me, though, and that's why, to this day, I don't have a cool beaver hat.

All night, Elle and Andy sat together and laughed through the movie. A couple of hours after everyone left, David came back to bum a cigarette off me. We stood in my cold garage as smoke swirled up and hit the ceiling. "So, what'd Andy say?" I asked.

"He thinks you're weird, but I told him, 'You get used to her.'"

CHAPTER THIRTY-FOUR

On Super Bowl Sunday, Angela and I went over to Andy and David's cabin, along with a few of their friends. The boys couldn't get the game to come in, so we spent the afternoon hanging around. Literally. We competed to see who could dangle from the ceiling beams the longest.

When it got late, I invited everyone over to our house to watch a movie or the satellite. Mom and Dad were out of town, so we could do whatever.

They said they were tired or they had to get up early the next day, but what I heard was, "Why would anyone spend more time with you than they have to?"

I meant for the invitation to be friendly, but I'm sure what they heard was an invitation to naked town. Because, as far as they knew, that was the main thing I did.

"*Whatever?*" Cole asked.

Cole was a little younger and a lot more arrogant than I was. We were the same height, with roughly the same body type—that type being the one that's so bony you might accidentally stab someone with your elbow. He was supposed to be a two-week houseguest at Elle's when I slept with him, but he'd screwed me over by sticking around.

I barely glanced over at him. "Fuck you."

"Been there. Done that."

No wonder Andy and his friend, Eric, didn't want to hang out with me. It was one thing for them to tolerate me tagging along with Angela or David, but it'd be a whole other deal if either of them chose to spend time with me of their own free will. I hadn't given them any reason to see me as anything other than "just some slut we know." I turned back to Cole and shrugged. "Fair enough."

That night I stayed up on the couch and watched TV. I couldn't sleep when Mom and Dad were out of the house. Every normal middle-of-the-night house noise startled me awake, and I felt like I owed it to Angela to stay up and guard the house. It was penance for not being there every night when she couldn't sleep in Arkansas.

But she still couldn't sleep well when our parents were gone, so she asked David to stay over the next night. She told him she was less scared with a guy in the house. I acted like I wasn't the least bit worried about staying alone, but I was glad she asked him over. I felt better with him there too.

When he walked through the front door that night, he told us to turn off the porch light and come outside. The three of us huddled on the front porch of the parsonage and stared straight up. A wavy green mist veiled some of the stars, and undulating green lines burst from a point right above us and shot out in every direction. An umbrella of light over our heads.

Our neighbors were probably watching us out their windows, wondering what the pastor's daughters were doing inviting some boy over to the house late at night when their parents were away, but I couldn't care less. I'd never seen anything like it.

"What *is* that?" I didn't even turn my head back down to David when I asked.

"Northern lights," he said.

I'd never heard of it.

When I was little, and we still lived in Texas, sometimes we'd have bonfires at night. I'd sit by the fire and stare straight up at all the stars in the wide-open sky. I never found another sky like a Texas sky, and it was the thing I missed the most about living there. There had been too much light pollution in Tulsa. In Indiana, we had the same problem. The trees in Arkansas blocked out most of the stars. But the previous summer's tornado had uprooted all the trees around the parsonage, and the sky here was just as wide-open as it had been in Texas.

Angela and David went back inside, but I stayed out on the porch, shivering because I hadn't bothered to grab my coat.

Green light danced over the new steeple. Snow, inches deep, piled up on the porch's handrail. Dark ruts in the yard marked the spot where I'd slid out of the driveway and plowed my car into a snowbank in our front yard last week. I hadn't gotten the hang of winter driving yet.

I shouldn't have been standing in the snow, staring up

at a green night sky. I shouldn't have been driving an hour on icy roads to a community college I was flunking out of. I shouldn't have been screwing whoever happened to be handy when I'd had a few drinks.

But there I was, standing still because I couldn't turn back. Because I was too scared to step forward. Because it was less heartbreaking to self-destruct than to try, and fail again.

CHAPTER THIRTY-FIVE

A bowling ball a few lanes over collided with the pins, and Elle smiled at me. "Who do you think has the best butt?" she asked.

I lit my cigarette and exhaled off to the side so I wouldn't blow smoke in her face. "I don't think about any these guys' butts."

"Except Cole's," she teased.

I didn't crack a smile. "*Especially* not his."

Since she'd started dating Andy, Elle had been dragging me along to bowling night, even though I was a terrible bowler. I only showed up to hang out with Elle and David.

Angela and I had grabbed a ride with David that night. I'd made it to the front passenger's seat ahead of Angela and made them both listen to Alanis Morissette for the whole twenty minutes it took to get to the bowling alley.

David sat down and grabbed my lighter off the table to light his own cigarette. "What're we talking about?" he asked.

I flicked my ashes into the tray. "Asses."

"Sweet!"

Angela took a seat beside David and immediately

started waving her hand in front of her face. "Stop blowing this way," she told me.

I glared at her. David was smoking right beside her, and I wasn't even exhaling in her direction. "Move to another seat," I said.

Every single time with her. She couldn't convince me to quit smoking, but she could sure badger me about it. Whatever comeback was on her lips was interrupted by the rest of the boys joining us: Andy, Eric, Josh, and Cole. Most of them took the whole bowling thing pretty seriously. Some of them even owned their own bowling balls and played on a league.

At the end of the first game, I had the lowest score, just like always. Between games, everyone wandered off to use the bathroom or buy something from the snack bar. I was the first back to the table, and lit up a new cigarette. I always chain-smoked at the bowling alley. I couldn't stand to sit there without something to occupy my hands.

Eric was the next person back, which was awkward, because he never said much to me. I'd only recently met Eric and Josh, and I hadn't known them long enough to get a good read on either of them yet.

"You should quit smoking," he said.

"Is the smoke bothering you too?" I waved my hand over the table to waft it away from him. I only gave my sister a hard time about it. I didn't want everyone else to choke on my secondhand smoke.

"No, but it's bad for you."

I stopped wafting and stared at him. "What difference

does it make to you?" I asked.

"I don't want you to die." He said it like it was the most obvious thing in the world.

He didn't want me to die? He'd known me for less than a month. People I'd known for years—people I'd loved—hadn't cared whether or not I died, though they'd have had a *huge* problem with me smoking. It wasn't a big deal if I got murdered, just as long as I didn't commit any sins on my way out.

The lesson I should have learned was that the people I'd gone to church with had some seriously screwed up priorities. Instead, I figured once people got to know me well, they stopped caring about me. Because there was something deficient about me, something inside of me that was fundamentally unlovable, and I had to keep people from getting close enough to see it. As long as nobody saw who I really was, I'd have a place here at two squished together tables, in a tiny bowling alley in northern Michigan.

"Don't worry. I'm hard to kill." I smiled at my little inside joke.

Angela set a can of Pepsi in front of me, and the rest of our group filtered back over to the tables. Elle leaned across the table to address Eric. "So, which guy do you think has the best butt?"

I figured I should save him, so I leaned forward and said, "I'm *definitely* the guy with the best butt around here."

CHAPTER THIRTY-SIX

Ankle-high snow crunched under my seasonally inappropriate tennis shoes as I made my way to Elle's garage. I stomped the snow off and shut the door behind me. Cole glanced my way, but he didn't stop swinging at the punching bag that hung from the ceiling. He must have thought it intimidated me.

"Sit," he said.

I stood. "If you've got something to say, say it."

He hit the bag and took a breath. "Why'd you say that shit to Desiree?"

Cole and I had been hooking up for over a month. His parents knew Elle's mom somehow. He was supposed to be a two-week houseguest, which was perfect for me, but then he decided to stay. I felt guilty because I hadn't known he was a virgin the first time we had sex. In my old world, virginity had meant something. I felt a little responsible for him, so I hadn't cut him off after one night, like I normally would have.

Our arrangement was simple and tilted in his favor. He got to have sex with me even though he was one of the most annoying people I'd ever crossed paths with. I only had one rule. He couldn't sleep with anyone else while he was sleeping with me. That was just basic human decency.

But the night before, I'd found myself wedged into Elle's back seat, between Cole and Desiree, as they flirt-fought over a plastic pixie wand until I blew up and shouted at Elle to stop the car so those two could get out and screw real quick so they could get it out of their systems and stop elbowing me in the head.

When we got to my house, I pulled Desiree off into another room and laid it all out for her. If she wanted him, she could have him. I'd back off. But flirting with him when she knew about our arrangement was messed up. Friends didn't do that kind of thing to each other. She told me she was sorry, and she wasn't interested in him that way, and then she told *him* that. Which was why he was now slamming his fist into a punching bag.

He raised his fist to punch again, and I said, "She was being a disrespectful little bitch."

He wheeled around to face me, fist still raised. "She's into me, and you chased her off."

I rolled my eyes at him. "I told her I'd back off, but she doesn't want you. She just likes the attention."

His fist reared back, like he was winding up to punch.

"Hit me or don't. It won't change anything."

For a second, I *wanted* him to hit me. It was the same feeling that terrified me sometimes while riding shotgun in a friend's car late at night. I'd find myself hoping we'd hit a patch of black ice. I didn't want to die, and I didn't want my friends to get hurt, but I knew if I were covered in casts and bruises, people would understand me better. It's easier for people to sympathize with pain when they can see physical evidence of it.

If Cole broke my nose or a flipped car broke my leg, people would come up to me and tell me how sorry they were I got hurt. They'd send me cards and buy me flowers and tell me how thankful they were that I was alive and they'd say, "Just let me know if I can do anything for you." But stalking victims don't get flowers or sympathy cards from their friends.

I always pushed those thoughts away as fast as they flooded in. It scared me to think about things like that. What kind of a person *wants* to get hurt? I didn't *really* want anyone to punch me. I didn't *really* want to be in a car accident. And I was horrified when my mind veered in that direction and fantasized about being a more palatable victim, even if it was just for that second before I caught myself.

Cole's arm dropped to his side. "I don't hurt girls."

A few days later, Elle staged a friendtervention. I was pissed at Desiree. Cole was pissed at me. Angela and David were bickering. Andy was there because we were all at Elle's house, and those two were dating, and Eric must have been caught in our gravitational pull because nobody was irritated with him, but he was there anyway.

We were supposed to sit there in Elle's living room and hash out our issues with one another while Elle facilitated. The conversation steered away from David and Angela and toward me. My real problem? Elle said I didn't let anyone get close to me. The circle nodded in agreement.

I sank into myself, folded arms and legs, taking up as little space as possible on the couch beside Angela. Elle told me I had friends who cared about me, and I knew she meant well, and maybe she even believed what she was saying, but it wasn't true. You had to know a person to care about them, and the only person in the room who knew me was my sister, and she *had* to care about me.

All the jokes I used to deflect any attempt to connect with me peeled off like scabs. I gave Elle a long, cold stare before dropping the mask just long enough to say, "You have no idea what it's like for me."

"Tell us," Elle prodded.

I shook my head. I couldn't. They wouldn't understand. "I mean it," I said. "You have no idea why I'm like this. You have no idea how much pressure's on me."

They probably thought I meant academic pressure, or moral pressure, since I was a pastor's kid. But I meant the pressure to survive. To never attract another stalker. To stay in control. To keep hidden so Ray couldn't find me and kill me or my family. To tiptoe around what happened so it wouldn't upset Mom or make Dad feel guilty. To carry around the guilt of having done whatever it was I'd done to put my family in that situation. To know that I was the reason my little sister was afraid to sleep in her own home. Pressure to pretend I wasn't homesick for the people who'd turned their backs on me.

My friends didn't know what it was like to stand outside at night, just smoking a cigarette and minding your own business, when you hear a squirrel run through fallen leaves, sounding exactly like a man sneaking up on you. And in that moment, you don't know if you should run or scream or cry or laugh because it's just a stupid squirrel, but some primal part of your brain doesn't understand that, so it keeps shouting, *You're about to die!*

Elle started to say something else, but Angela interrupted her with a stern, "No. Kristy's right. Our life's crazy. Y'all don't even know."

She told everyone to leave me alone, which led us to focus on Cole and his obvious low self-esteem instead.

I liked most of the people in that room, despite my best efforts to hold them at arm's length. I especially liked David, who might not have known all about me, but tolerated me amazingly well and never judged me, no matter what kind of stupid things I did. And I liked Andy, who never talked to me like someone who wanted to get into my pants, but opened car doors for me even when he knew it wouldn't get him anything in return. Eric hardly ever spoke to me, but when he did, it was usually to give me a hard time about smoking. Elle had been my first real friend in Michigan. They were nice to me, and I couldn't figure out why since all any of them got from me were bad jokes and secondhand smoke.

I liked them, but I didn't trust them. If I spilled my guts and listed all the sordid details, what would they do with that? Would they even believe me or would they think I was making it all up to get attention? Would they decide I was too much drama and drop me? Would they feel sorry for me and start treating me like a fragile little girl who could collapse at any minute?

How could I explain it anyway? As far as I knew, nobody had ever wanted to murder any of my friends. And the worst part wasn't even that Ray had wanted to kill me. The worst part was that my church council members would rather let him kill me than risk conflict within the church. How could I express what that felt like?

I didn't realize it then, but when you get right down to it, all pain is just pain. We've all been hurt by other people. We're all afraid sometimes. We all lose people we love. We're all *afraid* of losing the people we love. Everyone in that circle had been hurt by something or someone. None of them had been hurt in the same ways I'd been hurt, and a couple of them had barely been scratched by life at all, but the pain I felt wasn't some mysterious, unfathomable thing that none of them could've wrapped their minds around. It wasn't bigger than we were, but I guess that's one of those isolating lies we tell ourselves sometimes so we don't have to risk being vulnerable.

They said I had a problem, and they were right, but I didn't know what to do about it. I wished I could have rewound back to the person I'd been in high school. I wasn't the coolest person, but at least I was able to feel something beyond fear back then. At least I'd cared. Now, though, I didn't care about much of anything.

Sometimes Angela woke up that older version of myself, but she'd been through hell over the past year too, and you don't come out of that unchanged. What I needed was someone who'd known me before any binge drinking and chain-smoking and one-night stands. What I needed was Ben. He'd known me best when I was *at* my best. If I could talk to him, maybe it'd trigger something in me and I could reach back to salvage some better version of myself. And, even though I didn't want to admit it, I missed my friend.

A couple of nights later, I sat on my bed and dialed his number into the cordless phone. His mother answered. I asked for Ben, but didn't tell her who I was, hoping she wouldn't recognize my voice after a year of de-accenting myself.

Ben wasn't home. He was at the races, but did I want to leave him a message? "That's okay," I said, "I'll try him again later."

He was probably at the races with his new girlfriend. Angela and Daniel kept in touch. He told Angela he'd run into Ben at a mall a few months ago and saw him holding hands with a girl. I stepped into her shoes and asked myself if I'd be OK with my boyfriend's ex-fiancée calling him a year after their breakup. Probably not. It wasn't fair of me to conjure up ghosts for him, so I never did call back.

Two months later, I dropped out of school. Again. An online acquaintance I'd never met mentioned she was moving to Kansas City and needed a roommate. I chose to believe she wasn't secretly a sixty-year-old pervert and volunteered to move down. I needed a change. If I got out of Michigan, I could start over again and do it right this time.

Plus, it'd get me almost thirteen hours away from Mom and Dad. Since I'd dropped out, Dad said I had to pay my own way. I gave him $100 in rent each month, and bought my own food, but I still couldn't come and go as I pleased because staying out past 11:00 p.m. sent Dad off on a hollering tangent, like maybe he could shout me back to who I really was.

They didn't know what to do with me, and honestly, I didn't know what to do with me either. Objectively, I could see what I was doing, and I could predict the consequences of my "risky behavior", but I just couldn't stop self-destructing. It was a coward's suicide—long and drawn out—and it needed to stop.

I put in my two weeks' notice at the drugstore and showed up for a bonfire at Andy and David's to say good-bye to my friends. As we stood around the fire, I told the guys about my plan and made them promise not to forget all about me.

Once I got to Kansas, I'd get a job like the one I'd had in Indiana. I was pretty good with accounting, so something in an office, where I wouldn't have to wear a name tag.

After I was settled, I could start dating again. *Really* dating, not just hooking up. Maybe I was ready now. Maybe I just needed to push myself and give other peole the benefit of the doubt. Not *everyone* was dangerous.

After opening up a little about all my optimistic plans, I started backpedaling back into joke territory, where I was more comfortable. I went off on a rant about how I was moving away because there weren't any available guys in Comins, so I had to strike out and find love somewhere else. Since Andy and Elle weren't together anymore, and he'd always been nice to me, I told him I should probably just marry *him* and be done with it. I even got down on one knee in the sand and proposed, but he laughed and said no.

A little while later, he walked up to the cabin and back down to the fire with a green twist tie off a bag of bread. He twisted it into a ring and told me it was the man's job to propose, put the tie on my finger, and called me his fiancée for the rest of the night. We joked about our upcoming wedding for the next few days, until I packed up my baby-blue Topaz and headed south with two cartons of menthol cigarettes in the passenger seat.

CHAPTER THIRTY-SEVEN

The couch springs squeaked as I whipped my head back to drain my shot glass. The second my glass hit the coffee table, a boy with gelled hair and blue eyes filled it up again. And again.

The mason jar of moonshine in his freezer had freaked me out a little, and I was glad I chose Captain Morgan instead because I figured it took longer to get drunk with rum than moonshine. Of course, you're going to get drunk fast on anything when you're doing back-to-back shots.

He'd invited me to stop by because he was having a group of people over for a party, but nobody else was there. It was just me, him, and Captain Morgan. He was about my age, and he must have had an OK job because he didn't have a roommate. We had met a couple of hours earlier while I was smoking outside my apartment and he stopped to talk to me for a little while. I hadn't gotten to know anyone other than my roommate since I'd moved to Kansas, so when he invited me over it sounded like a good way to get to know some of my neighbors. But none of the other neighbors had shown up yet.

When I started listing off the couch, he stopped

pouring shots and pulled out a guitar. His arms were huge, and the guitar looked like a ukulele in them. As he played, his solid eye contact, searching for approval, irritated me a little. I wondered if he'd stop staring if I complimented him.

"You're good," I said.

He smiled and leaned in to kiss me. I wasn't aware of him doing it, but he probably set the guitar down first. I don't remember walking into his bedroom either, but there we were, and I was naked and underneath him. "Don't just lay there," he said.

At first I was mad at him for implying I'm not good in bed. My knee-jerk reaction was to wrap my arms around his neck to prove him wrong, but they were too heavy and dropped back onto the bed. Something was wrong.

He kept barreling ahead, and a thought cut through the fog. *I don't want to do this. Why am I doing this?*

I didn't remember agreeing to this, but I must have. Why else would I have been there? He was inside me, so I was already committed. *What sort of a bitch would back out now?*

He leaned his weight into me and groaned into my ear. "You're too tight. You're hurting me."

I was hurting *him*?

If it was painful for him, what did he think it felt like for me? And that got me fired up enough to burn off some of the rum. He should've realized I wasn't into it. He should've known I was too drunk for this.

I could tell him to stop, but what if he didn't? He was bigger than I was and stronger. He was crushing my chest, and I couldn't even keep my arms up. I couldn't *make* him stop, so maybe it was better to ride it out. He wasn't holding me down. He wasn't choking me or hitting me, but if I tried to push him off, he might. I didn't know if he was the kind of guy who would. I couldn't even remember what his name was, and there was nobody around to hear me if I screamed about a fire.

"Stop," I whispered.

He lifted his weight off my chest, but didn't stop moving. "Better?"

I raised my weak arms and pulled off my best shove against his shoulders. "Stop *everything*."

And he did.

Once he was off me, I rolled off the bed and crashed into a wall. He laughed like we were sharing a joke. "Watch out there," he said

My clothes were strung across the bedroom floor. I *never* threw my clothes around like that. Some of the guys I'd been with in the past had teased me about the way I'd carefully place my clothes in a pile because I never wanted to risk leaving without my underwear.

I gathered up my clothes and threw them on the best I could while making up some excuse about my roommate being worried if I didn't go home *right now*. She might even call the police, which I hoped would scare him enough not to grab me and fling me back onto the bed.

He followed me to the front door. When I turned the knob, he asked if I was really going to leave him with blue balls.

"Yeah," I said.

I stumbled through the halls of our apartment complex. I was so disoriented, I got lost once, wound up in the main lobby, and had to turn around. I passed "No Smoking" signs, but it was the middle of the night, so I pulled a smashed cigarette out of my back pocket, lit it up, and dragged on it as I lurched back and forth down the hall, swaying on Captain Morgan's ship.

Finally, after a couple more wrong turns, and a few bruises from smacking into walls, I made it back to my apartment and passed out on the couch without bothering to get undressed.

Two days later, I was smoking outside my apartment building when Mr. Blue Balls walked outside with a friend. The new boy stopped to chat me up while good old Balls kept inching away toward the parking lot. He barely even glanced sideways at me, which irked me something fierce.

I'd been willing to live and let live. I was drunk the other night. I assumed he was drunk too. At any rate, when I told him to stop, he did. But now he was pretending we'd never met, and that was some serious bullshit.

The friend told me our apartment complex was hosting a pool party that night for singles. He said they were going and wanted to know if I was going too. I told him probably not. A pool party sounded lame.

As the two walked off down the hill, Balls turned his head to whisper something to his friend, whose head made a sharp turn to stare at me for a second.

I knew what he'd just heard. "That's the crazy cock-teasing bitch from the other night."

I didn't like the way his friend stared at me. That streak of gratitude evaporated and swirled up with the menthol-flavored smoke I exhaled.

He may not have forced me, but it wasn't exactly consensual either. I wasn't comfortable putting any label on that night except one: *wrong*. What he did was wrong. When I had one-night stands, at least I made sure the guy was onboard, and I never hurt anyone.

Drinking with a stranger hadn't been the best idea I'd ever had, but I'd never had any problems with it before. I thought about that night in the bed of a truck, out in the woods, when a strange boy draped his coat over me.

Balls had poured shot after shot because he wanted me so drunk he could do anything he wanted. And I was obviously too drunk to actively participate. Things shouldn't even have gotten to the point where I had to say "stop."

It was the first time sex had ever scared me. I'd always had some amount of control every other time. Either I was with a boy I cared about and trusted, or I was with a guy who'd let me call the shots. The other night, some random asshole I'd met in a parking lot had called the shots, and I sure as hell didn't remember giving him permission to do that.

I was done with men thinking they could do what

they wanted, whenever they wanted, without any consequences. Ray had done it. J.R. had done it. Neither of them had been held accountable for it. I stubbed out my cigarette and went inside to tell my roommate I was going to a pool party.

CHAPTER THIRTY-EIGHT

When I was seventeen, our youth group leader decided to focus on Christian purity, which was really just code for virginity. Every Thursday night, she'd sit us all down and try to teach us how not to have sex, which is apparently a lot more complicated than "keep your pants on."

One huge issue in my church was female modesty. If anyone had bothered to check, we'd have known Jesus placed the burden of lust square on the shoulders of the person doing the lusting and not on the person being lusted after. He even told men to pluck out their eyes if they couldn't control their pervy thoughts. But some people in my church disagreed with Jesus on that one. They thought if a young woman flashed a little leg, no man in his right mind could resist the temptation. Because, as we all know, men are the more logical and less emotionally driven gender right up until they catch a hint of cleavage and suddenly morph into the sex-crazed primates we totally aren't related to.

So, all the responsibility for the world's lust got shifted over to us girls. We were responsible for what men felt and what they did because of those feelings. We had to keep covered up and say "no" if a boy tried to touch us.

My ankle-length skirt hadn't protected me from Ray. And my baggy sweatshirts and blue jeans hadn't protected me from J.R. I had a research notebook that said boys treated me the same way, no matter what I wore.

That's why, even though I was still uncomfortable about the other night, I didn't feel at all uncomfortable about walking around the pool in a two-piece. I wasn't vulnerable because I was wearing a bathing suit. I was vulnerable because I was a girl.

At least my mission had been successful. I'd been a big enough distraction to keep Blue Balls from hooking up with any girls from the party. I kept close by as he milled around; then I'd catch his eye while he chatted up some girl, and stare at him all wide-eyed with my eyebrows raised as high as I could get them. I was going for a creepy expression, but I think the fact that I was stalking him around the party was probably creepy enough.

My game was interrupted when a heavy arm wrapped around my neck. It was attached to a very tall, very sweaty, very drunk man. What he said was so slurred it took me a little effort to decipher it, but the general idea was he wanted me to go for a walk with him.

"Not right now," I said, hoping he'd plan on coming back for me later, and forgetting or passing out somewhere. I didn't want to deal with the scene a direct "get the hell out of here," would cause.

He squeezed my neck harder and tried to cajole me

into going with him. When I tried to duck out from under his arm, he squeezed again and took a step, pulling me with him. I gave a firm, "Get off."

The drunk guy opened his mouth, but another man's voice cut in. "Hey! Get away from her."

It was my wire-framed-glasses-wearing neighbor from across the hall, Keith. He and I had made eye contact a few times in the hall when we happened to be unlocking our doors at the same time, but we'd never even said "hi."

Drunkie didn't think it was any of Keith's business. He let me go, but only so he could throw a punch at Keith. He was too drunk to punch straight, and the swing went so wide I had to duck under his fist just before it would have caught me in the side of my head. I lifted my head from my crouched position a second later, but Keith already had the much larger guy pinned to the ground. One of the guy's friends came over and begged Keith to let him go and promised he'd take him home.

I stuck by Keith's side the rest of the night. He puffed up at the idea of being my personal bodyguard, and that was fine by me. Nobody had ever rescued me before. I guess I give off some vibe of being able to take care of myself. At least that's what Ben had always said when someone would mouth off and I'd ask, "Aren't you going to defend me?"

He'd shrug and say, "You do a good job taking care of yourself."

But I did a terrible job taking care of myself. I was doing shots in a stranger's apartment and stalking boys at pool parties. I was pretty sure I still needed some level of supervision.

When Keith invited me and another neighbor back to his apartment to watch a movie, I accepted because I never do learn my lesson. Instead of shots, he only gave me one drink, and he even mixed it in the only shaker I'd ever seen, which convinced me I was dealing with a legit grown-up for once. I asked how he'd pinned that guy, and it turned out he was a black belt, which sounded like something that'd come in handy with the way my life tended to go. Halfway through the movie, our other neighbor left, and Keith kissed me.

I was trying to turn over a new leaf, so I told him right up front that I wouldn't sleep with him. He said that was fine, but an hour later he'd pestered me so much that we were in his bed. But I wasn't drunk this time, so at least I could pretend I was in control again.

CHAPTER THIRTY-NINE

Three months later, I sat on Keith's couch and flipped through a benefits handbook. I'd just wrapped up a temp job for a hospital's HR department. That morning, I'd been offered a position in the accounting department, with full benefits and my own office. The department head handed me the handbook, told me to think about it, and let him know by Monday.

It was the first good break I'd had in a while. I was excited they wanted me. I hadn't been wanted for a long time. At least I hadn't been wanted for reasons that didn't involve being naked, and I was almost positive this job wouldn't involve me being naked.

Keith stood at the stove and stirred milk into macaroni noodles. "Have you ever heard of pet insurance?" I asked.

He hadn't.

"This is, like, a real job."

"All jobs are real jobs," he said.

I closed the handbook and held it on my lap. "I mean this could really be something. He said I could move up."

"Then take it."

It wasn't as simple as that, though. My roommate had

decided not to renew the lease, and I hadn't been scraping together enough money with temp jobs to cover rent anyway. If I were going to stay in Kansas City, I would need another place to live.

Keith wanted me to move in with him. He didn't think it'd make much difference since I spent most nights with him, anyway. It'd only be until I got situated, but how many people move in with their boyfriend and then back out after a few months? If I moved in, it would be a serious commitment.

He handed me a plate of macaroni and cheese. I inhaled it and was on my way back into the kitchen for more before he'd finished half of his. I'd had a bagel and coffee at my interview that morning, and nothing else since. It was hard to grocery shop when you didn't have the money.

I'd had a decent job for a couple of months, but then my boss had decided to leave the company, and my position as his assistant was eliminated. Not long after that, I woke up to an e-mail from Keith telling me to turn on the news because New York City and the Pentagon were under attack. For a few weeks after 9/11, the jobs dried up while everyone waited to see what would happen.

The less cash I had, the more time I spent with Keith, especially around dinnertime. When he made dinner for himself, he always offered me a plate, and some days that was my only meal.

My roommate was a nice person, and if I'd told her I just plain didn't have enough money to buy food, she'd have shared her own food with me. And sometimes she did when she made a big pot of pasta and chicken. But I hated asking for help without giving something back, and I was already going to be stiffing her on my half of the rent that month.

I could have called my parents and asked to borrow a little money until I had a steady job again, but that felt like too much of a failure. I wanted to prove I could take care of myself, and for some reason I decided getting my boyfriend to feed me counted as taking care of myself. Anyway, at least I wasn't taking advantage of him. He always got what he wanted out of me coming over, so I was "contributing to the household" if you looked at it that way.

It's not that I liked thinking of it like a transaction. I wanted to like Keith, and it wasn't exactly that I *didn't* like him. We just didn't have much in common. He thought movies like *PCU* were top-notch comedies. I'd sit on his couch and pretend to laugh at them while eating his spaghetti.

At least he had a good job, and he didn't sneak around with other girls. He had a double bed, which beat the couch I'd been sleeping on since I couldn't afford a bed yet. He never told me I was smart, but at least he said I was pretty, and I don't remember him ever being intentionally cruel about anything. Plus, he had a black belt and a bunch of martial arts weapons, which might come in handy if I picked up any new stalkers.

Bottom line: He was safe. I didn't have to worry about being alone, and I didn't have to try to navigate being single, especially with all the questionable decisions I tended to make when I was single. I didn't trust myself to be on my own.

It wasn't a one-sided deal, either. Keith got plenty out of the arrangement too. He was the kind of slightly built guy who'd probably gotten into karate to fend off bullies.

One weekend, he drove me to his hometown in west Kansas. I met his parents, like a girlfriend should, but then he took me to a high school football game at his old school. We kept moving around the bleachers so he could "see the game better," which meant walking up and down the steps or across the front of the stands with his arm around my waist or his hand in the back pocket of the cutoffs he'd asked me to wear.

The next night, we went up to his younger brother's house, just off his college campus. Because I was still underage, Keith packed me a water bottle of vodka for the fraternity party we went to. I spent the night playing the role of dumb, drunk blonde while he kept pointing me out to other guys as his girlfriend. When we left the party to stumble back to his brother's, I let him pull me behind some dumpsters for a little while.

As far as I cared, he could do anything he wanted. My rules were simple:

Don't hit me.

Don't cheat on me.

Don't buddy up to someone who wants me dead.

The mac and cheese must flow.

Was there anything more than that to any relationship? It wasn't like I had a lot of romantic ideas anymore.

We never talked about anything too serious. I gave him a vague outline of my family. Dad was a pastor. Mom stayed at home. A sister existed. He didn't know what shows I liked to watch, what my hobbies were, what books I read, or even what brand of pop I drank. But he did know what restaurants I enjoyed. And he knew I liked pineapple juice and Malibu rum.

A group of his old friends showed up the day after my interview. I came over straight from another temp job, wearing what I thought was a professional-looking blue dress. Mid-thigh. No cleavage. Hell, it had three-quarter sleeves.

Keith introduced me with his hands all over me, like always. I sat down and listened to them talk for a little while, then said I was going back to my place to change before we all went out for dinner.

As soon as I shut his front door, laughter roared up behind me, so I stopped and leaned against the cheap door. I couldn't make out everything they said, but I clearly heard " . . . that ass. You use those hips like handles?" followed by Keith's affirmation and more laughter.

For the first time in a long time, it wasn't my flight or freeze instincts that kicked in. My first thought was, *Who do these assholes think they're dealing with?* and I almost burst back into the apartment to let them have it.

But what would that accomplish? An end to my relationship with Keith? No more dinners. No place to stay. I was stupid for being angry, anyway. I knew he wasn't interested in me for my mind. But for him to encourage *other* men to see me as just some piece of ass was a step too far.

I called Keith from my apartment and told him I had a headache, so I wouldn't be going out with them. After the group left for dinner, I snuck outside to perch on the side steps and chain-smoke. I smoked one cigarette I couldn't afford after the other, and crushed each butt under my sandals. It was getting late, and my toes were starting to get cold, but I kept right on smoke-thinking.

What would my next move be? Taking this job wasn't just going to determine what career I'd wind up in. It'd determine the kind of life I was going to live. The kind of person I was going to be. Accepting the job meant moving in with Keith. Moving in with Keith meant making a long-term commitment.

Was I the kind of woman who was okay with being mentally passed around to her boyfriend's friends just so she'd have someone to watch bad movies with and eat prepackaged meals beside? Was I really the kind of woman who'd whore herself out for mac and cheese?

It had been two years since I'd left Arkansas. Two years of refusing to take control of my own life. Two years of blaming Ray or Jackie or Ben for backing me into this corner. Except I wasn't in a corner, and I hadn't been in one for a long time. I didn't have to be here. I didn't have to move in with Keith. I didn't have to stay.

It was easy to pretend I wasn't responsible for my situation. If Ray had left me alone, I'd have married Ben and been in my sophomore year of college instead of chain-smoking and trying to figure out whether or not to stay with my just-wealthy-enough-to-buy-pasta-based-foods sugar daddy.

I was still walking around like my life was being dictated by outside forces. I was waiting around for someone to swoop in to save me and guide me. But nobody was coming to save me. I was free to make any choice I wanted, and that was terrifying.

Ray wasn't deciding how my life went anymore. I had to take responsibility for my life and stop looking for someone else to take care of me. Keith wasn't taking care of me. He was using me.

I didn't need supervision, like I'd thought. I needed self-control. I needed confidence in my ability to set my own path.

The question wasn't what kind of woman *was* I but what kind of woman did I want to become.

I wanted to be the kind of woman who had a home. The kind of woman people loved and respected. Maybe I was too damaged to totally connect anywhere, but I did have a place where I was at least accepted, with people who gave a shit about me, even if I didn't understand why.

I had friends in Michigan. Real friends who told me to stop smoking because it was bad for me and asked me why I wouldn't let anyone get close and opened car doors for me. Friends who talked to me like a person and wanted to be around me because they thought I was funny, not because they thought they could get something out of me. Friends who knew me at my messiest and most ornery and gave me twist tie engagement rings.

After I stubbed out my last cigarette, I called Dad and asked him to mail me $200 so I could drive home to Michigan.

CHAPTER FORTY

It was a chilly spring day in northern Michigan. I couldn't get my car hood popped to add windshield washer fluid, and I needed that washer fluid if I was going to drive into Mio to rent a movie. The day before, I'd run out and had to drive home with a mud-and-slush-smeared windshield thanks to all the big trucks throwing melt up at me.

I was home alone, so I called Andy and David's cabin to see if one of the guys would come over and help. Andy came over within minutes. We'd been hanging out more often since I'd moved back. He and Angela had gotten to be better friends while I was gone, and I was glad he'd been around for her.

She told me about a night the whole group had gone bowling. One of the girls accidentally walked in front of a large man when he was about to bowl in his lane. She said she was sorry, but he started getting belligerent about it.

"It was amazing," Angela told me. "Andy just stood up and said, 'Hey.' That was it. All he had to do was stand up, and that guy started apologizing *real* fast."

A couple of days after he helped me with my car, I baked him some chocolate-chip cookies as a thank you, and he invited me to go bowling. At the end of the night, I hugged him good-bye, and one of us leaned in for a kiss, but we never did figure out which one of us leaned in first.

A few weeks later, David and I were driving back to the cabin with a pizza when a deer rammed into the side of my car and flew over the hood. We'd just passed Andy on the road, so I went back to get him because I didn't know what the hell you did with a half-dead deer in the road.

Andy pulled his white truck up along the side of the road. The deer's legs were broken, and it was calling out. Andy dug a hunting knife out of his truck. He strode over to the deer and pulled its head back, exposing its neck. He looked up at me then and said, "Sorry," but I was sitting on the hood of my car eating a slice of pizza.

Between mouthfuls, I told him to do what he needed to do. Why let anything suffer when you could prevent it? I'm pretty sure that's when he fell in love with me. And the fact that it even crossed his mind that I might be that tenderhearted (and I had been at one time) impressed me so much that I was sold on him too.

A few months later, Andy gave me a real engagement ring. I told Mom she could do whatever she wanted with the wedding plans. I was convinced Andy would wake up one morning and realize what a huge mistake he'd made, and I couldn't handle planning another wedding that wouldn't happen. I was itching to elope, but Andy's guest list was huge, so Mom bought me a big, white dress, and Andy's family fixed food for the reception while Mom baked and decorated our cake.

I stood in front of a sanctuary full of strangers, in a church that Mennonite Disaster Service had helped build while Ray was climbing through my bedroom window. I started feeling a little wobbly, but when I glanced behind Andy, David winked at me, and that almost started me off on a hysterical laughing fit because how the hell had I wound up there, in a brand new church, in front of all those Yankees, standing beside someone who knew all about my questionable reputation, but was still so excited to marry me, he'd picked the poem for our wedding invitations and printed them himself?

This was where I'd really start over. A new name. A new life. I thought I could put the past away and only focus on building a future with my husband.

Dad choked up as he prayed a blessing over us at the end of the ceremony. He walked up to me after everyone had hugged me and shaken my hand in the receiving line and said, "I'm real proud of you."

"What for?" I asked, because I hadn't done anything except show up. I didn't think it was that big of an accomplishment to get someone to marry you. People managed it all the time.

"For everything," he said, and he hugged me then, even though we aren't a hugging kind of family.

In the fall, I enrolled in school again. I was ready to be serious about it this time, and my grades showed it. My plan was the same as it ever was. Get my degree in education. Teach. Write. But a year later, Andy found a newspaper ad for a job closer to home and convinced me to apply. Not only did it pay better than the job I'd had, but it offered tuition reimbursement. The only catch was I had to get a degree in something useful to the company, so I switched to an accounting major. I mostly wanted to get the college degree I'd missed out on, and I figured I didn't really have the temperament for teaching anyway.

While I was in school, we had two daughters. Between working full time, doing homework, and having babies, I didn't watch prime-time television for almost five years. It took me that long just to get my associate's degree. Andy and Angela convinced me to drive down to Grand Rapids to walk during the graduation ceremony, even though I thought it was a waste of gas. Our car broke down halfway there, but we made it, and my parents, sister, in-laws, and daughters saw me walk. But I walked alone and I sat alone in the crowd of gray gowns because I didn't know any of the other graduates. It wasn't the college experience I thought I'd have when I sat on my twin bed at eighteen and highlighted all those interesting classes in UCA's catalog.

After our house was built, Andy and I sorted through some boxes we'd stored. I pulled out a teen devotional Bible, zipped up in a burgundy cover. In the front pocket, I found an old bulletin from Pine Creek Church. A note at the top said, "For your trip." A small notebook was shoved into the cover's pocket too. It was my old prayer journal, asking God to forgive me for that anti-courtship website and to please help me have more love in my heart for my fellow church members, even if I didn't always like what they did.

I hadn't touched that Bible in the past eight years. I hadn't thought much about my past in those eight years at all. While holding that Bible, I didn't think about all the hours I'd spent poring over it while preparing for one of the Bible studies I'd led. I didn't think about how excited I'd been when I walked into the Christian bookstore with the birthday money I'd saved up so I could buy it.

The only vision I saw was a teenage girl, on the day she left Arkansas, crying over an altar and praying for a miracle. A girl sitting alone in her dorm room, desperately searching the Word for some comfort and underlining James 1:2.

Consider it pure joy, my brothers, whenever you face trials of many kinds, because you know that the testing of your faith develops perseverance.

Once, while sitting on my bed, I'd accidentally knocked that Bible onto the floor and didn't notice until I woke up the next morning. I'd been horrified. God's word deserved better than my dirty laundry.

I stuffed the bulletin and prayer journal back into the front pocket and chucked the Bible into a black garbage bag. I glanced over at Andy. "Think I'll go to hell for that?"

He shrugged.

I lived my life and kept so busy I didn't have time to think about the past much. I checked the back seat of my car before getting in. I triple-checked the door and window locks each night, and I was a little jumpy, but

Ray wasn't actively on my mind. What Andy referred to as my OCD were just old habits—holdovers from when not doing those things might have gotten me killed. But nothing abnormal had happened to me for years, and I had a chance to focus on all the normal life stresses, like working overtime or trying to find that printout the pediatrician had given me because I couldn't remember how much Tylenol an eighteen-month-old could have.

Andy and I moved one town over. David moved downstate and got married. Josh, who I got to know better after I married Andy, joined the navy. Angela and my parents moved back to Indiana.

We didn't see everyone often. When Josh came back to Michigan over a Memorial Day weekend and brought his girlfriend, Janaye, most of us got together to go camping at Burt Lake.

The lake water was colder than I'd thought it'd be. I never had gotten it into my head that I lived in Michigan now, where summer came a lot later than it had in Arkansas.

Andy was sitting on the pontoon boat with our five-year-old daughter and David's four-year-old daughter, but almost everyone else was in the water with me.

At least they had been with me a second earlier.

I swam around to the end of the boat. Everyone was floating or treading water up under the boat's platform, between the two pontoons. "This where the cool kids hang out?" I asked.

It was so cold, and I wasn't the swimmer I used to be back when Angela, Daniel, Ben, and I used to head to the

Act Normal

river in the summer. A shoulder injury and those years I spent smoking hadn't done me any favors either. At about the time I made it under the boat, everyone else decided it was too cold for them too and swam back around, while I lagged behind.

I felt what I always feel—a little out of sync with everyone around me. I always put in a good effort, but I never could quite keep up. I'd been with this group for over ten years and I loved them, but I still felt like I was just circling the perimeter.

Since I was pretty sure I'd get hypothermia if I didn't get out of the water, I swam around to the side of the boat and watched everyone else hoist themselves up using two handles. When everyone was up, I swam over and grabbed those handles, but my shoulder hurt and even without that, I didn't have the upper body strength to pull myself up. Two pairs of hands reached down, grabbed my arms, and pulled me up onto the deck. I don't remember who pulled me up because it easily could have been any of them.

After the kids were asleep in their tents, we sat around the campfire, drinking and getting nostalgic. Eric asked if I still had that coat with the giant leopard print collar. I'd flip the collar up over my head and harass people about giving me a pumpkin for a new head. I hadn't worn that coat in almost ten years.

David brought up my old car. My first winter in Michigan, I'd driven an old wood-paneled station wagon with bald tires and a bad alternator, so I always had to unhook the battery each time I turned the car off. David and I told his wife about the time I came to pick him up at the cabin and the dam over the pond was so icy, we got stuck on it, sliding forward and then backward over and over because he couldn't brake and I was sure he was going to slide off into the pond.

Josh's girlfriend was there. And Eric's girlfriend. That weekend was the first time I'd met either of them. I tried to steer the conversation away from too much "old time" talk because I knew what it felt like to sit around with a group of people who'd known each other forever. You feel left out. It was how I'd felt when I first met those guys. Josh, David, and Andy had known each other as babies, and you can't compete with history like that.

You can't compete with it, but sometimes you can become part of it. It took me by surprise, even though it shouldn't have. I wasn't the new person, listening to all the old stories and wishing I'd been there. I was the person *in* the stories.

I hadn't wound up where I thought I would. I didn't marry the first boy who kissed me. I married the first boy who gave me a twist tie instead. I didn't live in the same small town where I went to school, and my friends didn't all live nearby and pop in for a visit, but I was sitting by the fire with people who'd known me longer than any other group of people had known me. I was with people who pulled me out of the water before I asked and who remembered things about me I barely even remembered myself.

I was with Josh, who showed up one night when Andy was out of town while I was struggling to load the wood stove by myself. He took the log out of my hands and started stoking the fire without a word about it. And Eric, who called looking for Andy one night, and when I told him I'd totaled my truck that day, said we could always get a new truck, but we couldn't get a new me. And David, who mysteriously managed to guess I was pregnant *twice* just by the tone of my voice over the phone.

I was always surrounded by low-level loneliness. I figured people couldn't really know me if they didn't know the worst parts of me, but that was bullshit. They didn't know every single thing about me, but they knew me. They thought I mattered, and maybe that was a miracle.

Part Four

**SEPTEMBER 2012
WASHINGTON**

I have told you these things, so that in me you may have peace. In this world you will have trouble. But take heart! I have overcome the world.

– John 16:33

CHAPTER FORTY-ONE

It was a picture of my old friend from youth group, Skittles. She was standing on top of the Seattle Space Needle, right there in my Facebook feed. Andy and I had just moved to Washington a few months earlier, so I messaged her. "Are you in Seattle right now?"

She was. We set up lunch for that weekend so I could meet with her and her girlfriend. The only time I'd seen any of my Arkansas friends was during a short visit in Little Rock five years earlier. On our way to Texas, we'd stopped off at a waffle house for about an hour to have breakfast with Louise.

The last time I'd seen Skittles had been thirteen years earlier, on my last night in Arkansas. She and I hadn't kept in touch. I'd only managed to stay in touch with Louise, but even that was sporadic. A phone call every couple of years. An e-mail here and there. It's hard to keep in touch with all your old friends when nobody is supposed to know where you live.

Over the past few years, I'd started to loosen up a little and joined MySpace and Facebook when they came out, though I didn't list my actual hometown. For a while, I used my maiden name, just to add one extra layer of anonymity, but that had the side effect of allowing my old friends from Arkansas to find me more easily.

Every time someone from Arkansas found me on MySpace or Facebook, it gave me a little jolt of anxiety. I doubted any of them would run off and tell Ray where I was. They probably didn't even know Ray. And I doubted any of them sat around, asking their friends, "Hey, what ever happened to that Kristy girl we used to go to school with?"

But there was always that small chance. So, I kept my hometown off all my social media profiles, took a deep breath, and confirmed their requests. I was tired of being in hiding. I was tired of not being able to talk to my old friends.

I even confirmed a friend request from Mike's wife, Rhonda. Mike had been an elder at the Pine Creek church. He'd let Ray stay at their home while everything was happening, hoping to provide him with a nightly alibi.

When I got the request, I thought she might be trying to check up on me. Maybe she felt a little guilty about how everything happened, and she just wanted to see if I was OK. I accepted her request and waited for a private message, but she never contacted me.

After a while, I felt uncomfortable with her having access to my profile, given her family's close friendship with Ray in the past, and the fact that she didn't seem interested in interacting with me at all. So, I removed her.

I didn't have to worry about Skittles, though. She

wasn't even living in Arkansas anymore, and she'd been like a little sister to me in high school, so I trusted her.

Andy dropped me off in front of her hotel, where I was greeted by the same bold red hair and sweet smile I remembered. She introduced me to her girlfriend, and the three of us walked a few blocks to a restaurant. She talked about the food there like someone who knew food, which was a little intimidating since I'm not exactly the most culinarily cultured person in the world. It was weird at first, like meeting with a stranger, because the girl I remembered was happy to adopt a candy-based nickname and hadn't traveled to Europe and didn't know how to pick a wine.

But she was still the girl I'd known. The girl who'd joined me for a lip sync competition we'd made up on the spot because we were bored at youth group one night. The girl who hadn't stopped me when I decided to try smoking a candy cigarette and who'd laughed along with me when we found out that sugar is super flammable.

Both of us loosened up a little, and after a while she filled me in on more of her history. At one point we both admitted to not attending church anymore, and it felt like the table's vibe lightened.

It was cathartic to hear her call our old church "toxic." A switch flipped inside me. Someone else had seen it for what it was too. It wasn't just me.

Skittles didn't feel like she had a place in church anymore, but sometimes she missed that connection with God. I didn't miss all the gossip or the judgment or the wacky theology, but I missed that feeling of being connected too. Of belonging to God and a community with a common purpose. It was comforting to know I wasn't alone in grieving for a place that wouldn't welcome either of us.

Over the next couple of days, our conversation stayed on my mind. She was one of the sweetest girls I'd ever known, and the pain from knowing you've been rejected and told God's for *those people*, and not for someone like you was something we both seemed to understand on some level.

But maybe it wasn't true. Maybe she and I *did* belong. We may not have belonged in *that* kind of church, but maybe there was a place for us.

On a bright Sunday morning, I parked at the far end of the lot and walked into the church alone. Just in case it was a crazy idea, I didn't want to inflict these people on my husband and daughters. The church was about the same size as the one Dad had been pastoring in Indiana for the past few years, though this one was emptier.

Fourteen years and a continental divide separated me from the church in Pine Creek, but that obituary Ray had left for me still followed me into every sanctuary I walked into. What if it happened again? What if I trusted these Christians and they threw me to a wolf? What if my daughters got hurt this time? I couldn't help being suspicious of any organized group of Christians I ran across.

I'd been talking to some people online since meeting with Skittles a few months back. Without my permission, I'd been added to a Bible discussion group on Facebook. I hung back for a long time, reading threads now and then, before point-blank asking, "Are you *sure* you want me in here?"

They all said they did, but then in the same thread a woman got so mad at me for saying people didn't get sick because of sin that she quit the group.

A lot of fundamentalist Christians hung out in there, and they drove me so crazy I went and bought a new Bible, just so it'd be easier for me to look up scripture to lob at them like grenades, which probably wasn't the noblest reason to buy a Bible.

Even though I'd read a lot of the Bible as a teenager, I needed a refresher so I could really show those fundies up. Reading the gospels as an adult turned out to be a very different experience from reading them as a teenager. Maybe you have to experience some suffering to really understand the gospel.

The gospel message was supposed to be joyful and hopeful and all sorts of other bubbly, sunny "fuls," but reading it now seriously bummed me out. Because I'd been cheated. This wasn't what I was taught by youth group leaders and Sunday school teachers. I was taught you had to accept a six-day creation story, or throw out the entire Bible. I was taught not to hold hands. I was taught to sing goofy songs and wear modest clothes and listen to Christian music and to never, ever utter a cuss word.

I wasn't taught grace. My church taught God rewarded the pure, not that Jesus came for the sick. For the suffering. For people like me. I wasn't taught that there was a place for me, even when I screwed up sometimes. Even if I thought evolution made a lot of sense. Even if I swore a lot and drank wine and wasn't a virgin when I got married.

A few of the nonfundamentalists in the online group talked to me about things. Communion and baptism and forgiveness. I read books that taught me how to read the Bible honestly without always reading it literally. I learned to recognize genre, which gave me a deeper appreciation for the book I'd ignored for most of the past fourteen years. Once I got past the idea that the Bible was either the literal word of God, zapped into existence, directly from heaven, or a total lie, I was much more comfortable with it.

I still wasn't a big fan of Christians, though. The biblical literalists in the group accused me of "forsaking the assembly" because I didn't attend church. They said it didn't matter if Christians had hurt me in the past. I was ignoring the clear commands of God by not attending church on Sundays. I thought they were full of shit. And they were.

Maybe God did want me worshiping with other Christians. Maybe he even wanted me to be doing that inside a church building. But where was the love and grace in demanding a wounded person leap headfirst into the trap that wounded them in the first place? Where was the recognition that it's a huge burden to place on someone's back? Like those hypocrites Jesus rebuked, who placed burdens on others that they weren't willing to carry themselves.

Still, I did miss being part of a church, and it'd been a long time since I'd tried one, so I did a Google search for churches in my town. I disqualified any church with "inerrancy" in their statement of beliefs, and I also narrowed my search to churches with female ministers. I didn't mind male ministers, but if a church had a woman behind the pulpit, I figured there was less of a chance I'd run into any of that "the husband is the head of the wife, so submit already, you man-hating, feminist Jezebel" stuff.

A little ELCA church caught my attention. Dad called them progressive Lutherans. Small congregation. Female pastor. Lutherans would probably be OK. My grandpa was a Lutheran, and I'd visited his churches in Texas a couple of times, so I knew they didn't do anything too wild and crazy.

An older woman greeted me when I walked inside. She guided me into the sanctuary and apologized for how small the congregation was. As it turned out, the pastor was new. When the church hired a female pastor, all the members who had an issue with that left for the other Lutheran church in town.

I sat in a back pew and observed. The usher, and the only man in the sanctuary, invited me to take Communion when everyone else went up to the rail, but I said maybe next time. I hadn't taken Communion in fourteen years, and I wasn't going to just waltz up there and eat a cracker with a bunch of strangers.

After the service, my greeter invited me to stay for coffee and snacks in the Fellowship Hall. I sat down at an empty table with my paper plate full of cheese crackers and my overly sugared coffee. Almost every woman in the hall descended on my table, borrowing chairs from neighboring tables and crowding in.

A middle-aged woman with close-cropped hair asked, "What are you, anyway?"

I laughed along with the other women at our table. "You mean what denomination?" I asked.

That was what she meant.

I told them my father was a Mennonite pastor, and quickly added, "Not *that* kind of Mennonite," when I noticed some surprised expressions and remembered the local Mennonites were more conservative than my family was.

But this woman still thought I was being incredibly rebellious by visiting a Lutheran church. Her father was a Southern Baptist preacher, and she immediately adopted me as a kindred spirit because we'd both moved past the fundamentalism of our youth and landed in an affirming church that Sunday morning.

Another woman filled me in on the church's recent past. They'd had a large youth group, but something had happened with the youth pastor a year ago. "Not a sex thing," she assured me, though she didn't elaborate.

I heard about the boy who used to play drums on

Sunday morning. One Sunday, he wore a ball cap up front and some "old bitty" gave him a hard time about it, so he stopped coming to church, but she was gone now, so they didn't have to put up with her crap anymore.

They weren't what I'd expected, and I wasn't sure what to do with that. I'd never heard people talk about their church the way this group of women did. Their church was flawed, but they didn't even try to hide it. To top it off, they said "damn" and "hell," and they weren't even telling me where I'd go if I didn't straighten up.

A few Sunday visits later, I sat on Pastor Shelly's couch, drinking tap water and asking if anyone would give me a hard time about my daughters not being baptized.

She mentioned something called radical hospitality, which was all about meeting people where they were, not where we thought they ought to be.

"I haven't been to church in a long time," I admitted. I cut eye contact with her and stared at a cross on her living room wall. "I had a bad experience when I was younger." I didn't explain it further than that.

There was no judgment from her. No lectures about forgiveness or how I should get over whatever it was and obey the clear instructions in the Bible. No talk about "God's plan" and how I should lie back and go with God's flow. Just more "radical hospitality."

Somehow, we got onto the subject of the crucifixion. I copped the uppity tone I use when I know I'm about to impress people with how spiritually mature I am, and complained about how obsessed some people were with the crucifixion. It was creepy and morbid. "We should focus on the living Christ," I said.

Shelly smiled and reminded me that the crucifixion was important too. "We have to walk through Friday to get to Sunday," she said. We couldn't have Christ's resurrection without Christ's suffering.

What really got to me wasn't the idea that Christ had suffered for my personal sins, which were both numerous and creative. I wasn't sure if I even believed Jesus *had* to die to erase my sins, since I was still building my theology back up one brick at a time.

What hit me was the idea that Jesus was God. It was something I'd known I was supposed to believe, but that whole Trinity thing didn't make a lot of sense, and I didn't understand why it mattered. Turns out, it matters a lot. Because if Jesus is God, then God himself came to earth to live as one of us. To suffer as one of us.

I used to think if we could just figure out the right combination of words and actions, we could avoid suffering because suffering was a punishment for screwing up and not being perfect as our Heavenly Father is perfect. But Jesus was perfect, and he suffered anyway. Maybe I needed to rethink some things. Maybe Harold Kushner had it right, after all. Sometimes bad things happened in my life because I made bad decisions. But sometimes bad things happened independently of anything I'd done. On some level, I knew that innocent people suffered in the world, but I'd never quite been able to apply that idea to myself. I figured I *must* have done something to deserve it, because if I hadn't, then the world didn't make any sense. But what sense did it make for God to allow himself to be tortured and killed?

I reread the crucifixion accounts in the gospels. God was abused by his own creation. By people he loved. I'd felt so distant from God, like I was the outcast of the Christian family and God the judgmental, out-of-touch-with-kids-these-days father. How could someone as big as God understand how I felt?

He could understand because he'd made himself small. If anyone knows what it's like to be betrayed by the people you love and endure pain and humiliation at their hands, it's God. God wasn't the last one who could understand what I'd been through. God was the *only* one who could fully understand how I felt. Jesus on the cross was my God: the God who suffers.

The next Sunday, I brought Andy and the girls with me. I walked up to the rail with the rest of the congregation, kneeled, and held my hands palm up for the wafer.

CHAPTER FORTY-TWO

There weren't any ELCA churches close to us when we moved back to Michigan, so I stopped going to church on Sunday mornings. But I didn't stop reading about Christianity, and I kept talking to other Christians online.

I got it into my head that Catholics were the strictest Christians of all, and when a Catholic friend told me that Catholics were totally fine with evolution, that sealed it for me, and I knew I was officially back in the club. From there I started rebuilding my faith, which was a much longer process than I'd anticipated.

People around me had always said things like, "God won't give you more than you can handle." That kind of thinking presented a huge hurdle. First of all, people get more than they can handle *all the time*. I sure couldn't handle Ray.

If I was "given" a traumatic experience, that certainly didn't come from a loving God. God might allow evil things to happen sometimes—possibly to serve some purpose—but he doesn't *cause* evil things to happen. He doesn't *give* us evil.

After I decided God wasn't to blame for my situation, I started trying to figure out the big theological questions, but that was overwhelming. So, I settled on a few basics, starting with Jesus. I believed in Jesus, and because of that, I believed I should do what he said. He had a lot to say about how we should treat other people, even people we don't like. Even people who don't like us. Even people who wouldn't mind if we were dead. But I'd spent fifteen years building emotional and spiritual fortifications, and the thought of knocking them all down scared me.

After Christmas, I sat on a couch across from Janaye while she held her new son. We talked about anxiety, which was an odd topic for me. I didn't like to admit I was anything other than One Badass Bitch You Don't Wanna Mess With.

But Janaye's one of those rare people with X-ray vision, who cuts through all my bullshit, so there was no point in pretending.

"I've had panic attacks before," I said.

She asked what triggered them.

I thought about an incident from half a year ago. I'd almost thrown up in my office while reading a breaking news story about a blonde teenage girl who'd been kidnapped by her father's friend after he killed her mother and brother and set them on fire.

I was quiet for a minute and stared off into the kitchen. I hadn't said it out loud for years. "A long time ago, I had a stalker. So, things that remind me of that. Sometimes."

"Kristy, that's PTSD."

I turned back to her and sighed. I liked to think the

things I'd gone through had toughened me up and made me strong, but it wasn't true. Strong people didn't obsessively check their door and window locks multiple times every night.

"I know."

She was the first person to acknowledge that something from my experiences had stayed with me. She didn't expect me to be OK just because I got away. Yes, I'd survived Ray, but survival wasn't enough.

A few months later, I sat down and wrote a long blog post about Ray. I didn't post it because I was looking for someone to pat me on the head or offer their belated condolences. I wrote it because I'd been blogging about my spiritual wandering for a while, and it kept bubbling up in my posts. My journey didn't make any sense if I withheld that part of my past.

I was scared to get into the details. People would wonder what I'd done to attract him. They'd think I was making a big deal out of nothing. I'd get comments about how stupid I was for letting something that happened years ago keep me out of a pew today.

I put up the blog post, threw a link to it up on Facebook, and waited for all the judgmental comments to start rolling in. I figured most people would ignore it, a couple would say something like, "Sorry that happened," and at least a few would take some sort of jab at me. *Why can't you just forgive and forget?*

A few hours later, I had nothing but supportive and encouraging comments. People I went to high school with told me they were proud of me. People I'd never met before told me they'd been traumatized in their churches too, and they understood how it felt. I never did get any of the negative reactions I'd expected.

It took me a while to understand what I'd needed for so long was validation. I needed to hear that what had happened to me was wrong, and I needed to hear it from Christians. I couldn't forgive anyone without first acknowledging the pain they'd caused me.

That simple validation gave me the space I needed to start letting my defenses down. Once I heard it was OK to be angry, that anger started to cool off. Years before, I'd wanted Ben to get angry, on my behalf, so we could share that burden. I was right back then. When I saw how indignant other people were *for* me, it eased that yoke off my shoulders. Instead of bearing that entire weight on my own, other people were now carrying some of it with me. I wasn't alone anymore.

I decided that being a peacemaker was a Christian's role and recommitted to pacifism. But this was a new kind of pacifism for me. It didn't mean standing still while someone repeatedly punched me in the face. That wasn't what Jesus wanted. We shouldn't fight violence with violence, but that doesn't let us off the hook when it comes to fighting it. We just fight it in a different way. It's the trap so many pacifists fall into. We think we can avoid violence by avoiding conflict and not getting involved. We forget that silence can be a violent act.

That was the sin so many of my old church members had committed. They'd tried to remain neutral, but when you're faced with evil, there is no neutral. When you don't speak up against violence, you've chosen to side with it.

I figured I'd begin my new life as a non-passive pacifist by starting with prayer. If I'm working to promote justice, but I'm not praying for peace, I'm only doing half the job. I started praying daily for peace, though my prayers went something like, "God, please bring us peace—just don't bring it *here*!"

Reaffirming my faith had surfaced all sorts of buried resentments. I didn't know how to be anything but angry. If I wasn't holding onto that anger, it felt like I was letting my old church off the hook.

While reciting the Lord's Prayer, I kept getting hung up on "forgive us our sins, as we forgive those who sin against us." Had I forgiven those who'd sinned against me? Not by a long shot.

I had never prayed for my enemies. I'd advised other people to pray for *their* enemies, and I'd gotten all high and mighty about how revolutionary it was for Jesus to give us those instructions. When you pray for someone, it humanizes them, and they stop being an enemy. And that's *exactly* why I refused to pray for anyone at Pine Creek Mennonite Brethren. I didn't *want* to humanize them.

One night, while I was praying for peace for everyone in the world *except* those people at Pine Creek Church, I stopped. Suddenly, I wondered what they were doing now. In my head, they were all stuck in 1999. A lot could have happened to them since then. Maybe some of them had realized the mistakes they'd made. Maybe some of them had changed. Maybe some of them felt guilty about what they'd done, or what they *hadn't* done. If there was even the possibility they could repent—the possibility of some future reconciliation—didn't I owe it to all of us to get the ball rolling? And what better way to do that than through prayer?

I couldn't bring myself to pray blessings their way, so I started praying for our spiritual healing instead. That was a huge step. By praying for spiritual healing, for all of us, I was really praying for reconciliation. Up until that point, reconciliation had been impossible because *I'd* been unwilling to entertain the idea. Now, it would be up to them. I didn't have much hope for it, but at least it was possible now. And I think that's really what being a peacemaker is about. It's about opening the door. I hadn't quite forgiven as my sins had been forgiven, but I'd opened the door.

One afternoon, I typed a Facebook message to Rev. Melissa Fain, a Disciples of Christ pastor I'd met online. She'd quickly become a cross between a friend, a pastor, and a forgiveness mentor for me. One of my first interactions with her was when she'd invited me to write for an Advent devotional, which surprised me at the time because I cuss a lot on my blog, and she read that shit, so I don't know *what* she was thinking. Being invited to participate in that way moved those rusty gears in my head forward a little more. The ELCA church had been the first place I'd felt welcomed by Christians. Fig Tree, with Rev. Melissa, was the first place I'd felt *wanted*.

She was generous with me because she understood. She'd been burned by a church too, though she seemed to have handled her injury more gracefully than I'd handled mine.

I'd been writing a lot about Ray and the Pine Creek Church lately, and we were talking about my latest blog post. I wished I'd started working on forgiveness earlier, but I was slow. I told her fifteen years was way too long to exile myself to the wilderness. She reminded me the Israelites had wandered the desert for forty years, so maybe I should cut myself a little slack. I didn't have to be perfect, and I didn't have to forgive all at once.

I wanted to forgive them, but I didn't understand how to do that without justifying what they'd done. I thought maybe I could work toward forgiving them if I understood them better.

My plan had always been to write about what happened. When we first moved to Michigan, I'd sat down at my computer half a dozen times and started writing, but listing out everything that had happened was too big of a thing for me to meet head on when I was still so close to those events. After a couple of false starts, I gave up.

Two years into my marriage, I decided to give writing another go. I called Dad and asked him to mail me the evidence folder. My parents had kept every note, magazine page, and Bible page Ray had left.

Dad said the folder was gone. He and Mom had a talk when they'd moved back to Indiana and decided to get rid of it because they felt like it was time to move on.

"Nobody asked if *I* was ready to move on," I said, but it didn't matter because it was already done.

Again, I dropped the whole idea of writing about it. I didn't think I could write about what had happened without all the evidence sitting in front of me.

But I was wrong. Fifteen years after leaving Arkansas, I started writing again, and I realized the story wasn't the crime story I'd been trying to write for so long. And it wasn't a hero story—me against Ray or me against the church. It was a story about people being people. Sometimes normal, average, kind, and generous people stand by and let horrible things happen.

Writing about what had happened from the perspective of an adult gave me a new take on it. When I was a teenager, I saw everything in black-and-white terms. This was right. That was wrong. As an adult, I knew it was more complicated than that. People sometimes do evil things with good intentions.

I was curious about Ray. I needed to know what happened to him. Did he stalk some other girl after I left? Kill her, maybe? I did a little digging online and found out he got remarried a few years after I left. Then he was charged with domestic violence and his wife divorced him. She even got a restraining order.

I was torn between feeling guilty about not stopping him before he got to this other woman and feeling vindicated. Jackie had said it couldn't possibly be Ray, but here was proof that he was violent. How could it be impossible for him to hurt *me* when he'd hurt his wife? I wondered if Jackie knew his wife. Had she seen her bruises? Had Mike or Elmer? Had Ben?

While sorting through old pictures from my parents' garage, I found some folded up sheets of paper. I stared down at underlined Bible verses. Dad had made a few extra copies of the Bible pages Ray had left, and they'd been shoved into a box that hadn't been fully unpacked since we'd left Arkansas.

When I'd written that blog post about Ray a few months earlier, I'd been worried that my memory might not have been as accurate as I'd thought. Maybe it hadn't really been as bad as I remembered. Maybe I'd blown it out of proportion over the years. But I looked down at the page in my hand and saw the exact same verses underlined that I'd quote in my blog post. Fifteen years later, and I could still quote Ray. These things really had happened. If anything, I'd underestimated the danger I'd been in at the time. As an adult, I could better understand exactly what it was he'd planned to do to me.

Mom was sitting with me, so I quickly folded the pages up again. I knew seeing them again would upset her, and the fact that I was blogging about all of it and dredging up all those old memories was upsetting enough. So, I took the pages home with me. I'd look them over on my own.

When I pulled into my driveway that afternoon, I stayed out in the car and unfolded the pages. My daughters peeked out the living room window at me, but

I couldn't read those pages around them. I didn't want any part of Ray touching their lives.

I expected a panic attack, but it didn't come. I read over the verses again. They were the pages he'd left in my bedroom the night he set my bed on fire. I was so young and terrified and lost back then, but I wasn't any of those things now.

A couple of months later, I decided to strip those threats bare. I scanned parts of the underlined verses about swords and burning down houses and ending prostitution and gave them the MST3K treatment on my blog. Every threat got a joke. How could I be afraid of something while laughing at it?

It helped some, but it didn't erase the pain. I needed to understand how this could have happened. I needed to know it wasn't my fault. On Easter morning, I sat at my parents' dining room table and half-jokingly asked Dad if he thought people in the Pine Creek Church had been so scared of the Y2K bug they'd wanted to run us off because they didn't want us in their new utopian society. He told me several of them had been listening to a man who'd been a guest on a popular Christian radio show in the '90s.

I didn't remember hearing of this man before. He was an author and popular with some of our church members. His old website from the 1990s was gone, but when I looked it up in the Way Back Machine from Internet Archive, I found dire Y2K predictions dating from the late 1990s. It also brought me to a series of old newsletters he used to send out and books he'd written.

I recognized some talking points in those newsletters. Stockpile. Move to the country. The end of civilization is almost here. People from my church said those things, and now I knew where they'd gotten those ideas from.

This man was, and still is, a leading voice in the Christian Reconstructionist movement. I did a little research and learned Christian Reconstructionists are working to build a theocracy that will hold to Old Testament law, including Old Testament punishments for breaking those laws. Late one night, as I read through a list of laws they wanted to implement, vomit rose to the back of my throat. Right there, on my monitor, was one of the verses Ray had underlined and left for me, just weeks before setting my bed on fire: Leviticus 21:9.

If a priest's daughter defiles herself by becoming a prostitute, she disgraces her father; she must be burned in the fire.

My daughters were playing in the living room, so I snuck back to my bedroom, shut the door, and had a decent cry. For a little while, I felt like I was eighteen again and Ray could show up at any second with a lighter. Even though I knew I was safe and I had good locks and I hadn't heard from Ray in fifteen years, the part of my brain that lights up during a panic attack told me I was about to be murdered, and it took a while for it to shut up again.

After that, I got a little obsessed with researching Christian Reconstructionism. I read old newsletters written by people who said disobedient children should be stoned to death. Also, people who are gay, people who commit adultery, and fornicators. The community should root out those evildoers or suffer God's wrath. God *wants* the community to participate in executing those who break his law. Low-level nausea accompanied me during every dive into that world.

In 1999, when people with a limited understanding of computers were worried that a small glitch would end civilization, the thought of replacing our secular society with a theocracy must have been awfully tempting. The people in my church would have been the new leaders of our community, and power is seductive.

I can't say how many of my former church members thought I deserved to die for having sex, and I don't even know if anyone other than Ray knew I had been having sex. And I don't know how Ray knew, but judging by the scriptures he threatened me with, it's obvious he found out somehow. Maybe he followed Ben and me one night when we parked down some back road and saw us fooling around. Maybe one of my friends or Ben's friends slipped up and said something that got back to Ray.

What I do know is Ray latched onto these beliefs and thought I deserved to die for my sins, though his beliefs were also complicated by his delusions—the ones caused by a mental illness that had supposedly been prayed away.

I don't know exactly what everyone else believed, or to what extent they believed it. Were they just worried about Y2K or did they wholeheartedly believe our country would be better off following Old Testament laws?

Did a theocracy just sound good to them on paper, or did they understand that theological beliefs aren't just theoretical, but have real-world impact? If Jackie knew what I'd done, did she think I deserved to be burned alive? Did Elmer? Did Mike, when he called me "precious," also believe whores should be burned to death because the Bible says so? Did anyone think Ben deserved the same death that I deserved?

Who should I blame? *What* should I blame? I wanted some definite answer. I wanted to be able to say this, *this right here*, was what happened. This was why things got so bad. It wasn't that simple, though.

Our church focused too much on sexual purity, and not enough on spiritual discernment. If we'd focused more on the spiritual gift of discernment, nobody would have been reading newsletters from Christian Reconstructionists. And they would have seen Ray for what he was—a man with a serious mental illness who needed both prayer *and* professional help.

The way leadership worked in our church contributed too. Dad was the pastor, but Elmer had been there long before us, and he was always the *real* leader. It's a common problem in small churches. Why would anyone risk standing behind a temporary pastor when they'd have to deal with Elmer after Dad was gone? And Elmer's family filled the church council, so the whole ordeal turned into an old-timey family feud on top of everything else.

Greedy men who hyped up the Y2K scare for their fifteen minutes of fame didn't help either. Some of our

Act Normal

church members were convinced Y2K would wreak havoc on our country's infrastructure, and fear can twist people's hearts in ways nothing else can. Maybe if they hadn't been so preoccupied with all that, they'd have seen things more clearly.

Nobody's afraid of Y2K now, but we still see the same fear-mongering tactics at work today. The war on Christmas. The secularization of our schools. Christians will be discriminated against for discriminating against others. It's all about fear. But the message of the gospel isn't fear. It's love, and love drives out fear.

Some people take advantage of that fear. They don't preach love. They preach hunkering down and looking out for yourself. If someone is fed harmful theology, how responsible are they for acting on it? Was it all Ray's fault, or do the men who taught Christian Reconstructionist beliefs bear some responsibility too? Does some of this fall on the members of my church who let men like Ray off the hook by idolizing virginity and blaming women for tempting men and "causing them to stumble?" How about the church members who told Ray he didn't need to see a psychiatrist because his schizophrenia had been healed through prayer?

How much responsibility rests with my church council members? If you don't harm another person, but you stand by and watch someone else hurt them when you could stop it, isn't that wrong too? Is there any such thing as an innocent bystander when something so blatantly evil happens in front of you?

My research didn't give me answers to those kinds of

questions, but it did cool my anger. I don't know how to forgive people who are willing to let me die, but I do know how to forgive people who were tricked into believing horrible things. I can forgive people who made decisions they might regret now, even if they'd never tell me that to my face. So, I started there.

Epilogue

**JUNE 2015
PINE CREEK, ARKANSAS**

Dear children, let us not love with words or speech but with actions and in truth.

– 1 John 3:18

Angela pulls up next to two cars in the Pine Creek Church parking lot as I check my makeup again. I don't want to stride into this place after sixteen years with streaky sweat marks all over my face.

I cut Angela off as she walks toward the front steps, reach the double doors ahead of her, and pull one open before I have time to chicken out. It feels important to go first.

The foyer smells like mildew. In the sanctuary, three older women sit in two pews and chat. For some reason, I lean forward and squint, even though I know exactly who I'm staring at. It's Ben's mother. "Ida?"

"Yes?" she says, with a politely detached smile. She can't place my face.

"We're Kristy and Angela . . ."

Three suddenly wide-eyed women stare at me. All at once, we're being asked how long it's been and where our parents are. I dodge the questions and tell them we've stopped in to see the addition.

"Right. We built that after you left," Ida says.

"There was a roof and studs when we left," I say, correcting her.

I think back to a few days before my family had given up our home here to escape Ray. After a day of packing up boxes, I found Dad working on the church roof that evening. I climbed the scaffolding until I was level with the roof and scowled at him. "Come down," I demanded, "Why bother?"

He looked over at me and said, "Because I made a commitment to get this roof finished. And I don't care what *they* do. I honor *my* commitments." Then he started swinging his hammer again.

Paul walks in. He'd been an elder during our problems with Ray. Unlike the women, he recognizes us right away. "Well, look who's here!" he exclaims, walking down the aisle toward us.

"Do you know who we are?" Angela asks.

"I know exactly who you are."

He envelopes Angela in a welcoming hug, then releases her and turns to give me one as well. Paul offers to play tour guide and leads us into the Fellowship Hall. At least it had been the Fellowship Hall sixteen years earlier. The old hall has been converted into classrooms.

This is where I led Bible studies. Where we "slept" during lock-ins. Where we whispered secrets and played quarter bouncing games with pop. Now, it's a string of empty rooms.

We turn a corner, and Paul leads us into the new Fellowship Hall—the one we helped build. The walls are covered with rustic, horizontal paneling, and a stone fireplace with an inlaid cross sits at the far end of the hall. Paul says Elmer brought those stones back from a mission trip in Turkey. Each stone of the cross represents one of the early churches.

I point to the slightly vaulted ceiling. "Somewhere up there's the truss I dropped on my foot."

Angela's more generous in her praise. She pulls out her phone and takes a few pictures to show Mom and

Dad. She asks, "Do you have a lot of kids in Sunday school?"

Paul sighs. "We don't have a lot of *anybody*."

He stops walking and does something shocking. He fills us in. The last pastor's wife got "infatuated" with Jackie's husband, which is Christianese for "they had an affair." At first I think he's talking about Scott, but then I remember I heard Jackie and Scott split up years ago, so this must have been a different husband.

When the pastor divorced his infatuated wife, the church fired him since they couldn't have a divorced man pastor the church. He had to pay the price for his wife's sin. Just like I'd had to pay the price for Ray's. That pastor left to start a new church, and took most of the congregation with him. Only a handful of members stayed behind.

It's the price of legalism. You sacrifice people who are suffering to keep to the letter of the law.

We express our sorrow, and surprisingly, I mean it. I don't want another pastor's family to be hurt here. Though, it does make me feel a little validated to know it hadn't just been us who'd run into trouble in this church.

Ben has taken over as the pastor. I don't know how that happened. I'd never thought of Ben as the pastoral type. Paul tells us Ben had a stroke a couple of years ago, though he isn't even forty yet. He's still preaching, but he has some trouble with his left side.

Elmer passed away three weeks ago. It strikes me how odd the timing of our visit is. Angela and I had sixteen years to come back, and we'd never wanted to. But for the past couple of months, we've both felt a strong pull to come back to our old hometown.

We follow Paul into the sanctuary, where the double doors open and two women walk in. One of them is Jackie. She's smaller than I remember, but I can't be any taller than I was back then. She spots us standing at the front of the church, and her eyebrows hit her hairline.

"Look who's here," Paul calls to her.

She doesn't blink as she walks straight to Angela and gives her a hug. "You're—" she sputters.

"Kristy and Angela," Ida finishes.

"Right. Robert's girls. I'm not so good with names."

I choke down the cynical little laugh that tries to burst out. I attended this church for four years. I sat on her couch and babysat her sons. I was engaged to her little brother. She sided with the man who wanted to murder me, and she was instrumental in running me out of this church, but she expects me to believe she doesn't remember my name.

She gives me a stiff hug, and I feel a pang of pity for her because there's no way she ever expected to see me again and face the possibility of being confronted with what she'd done, so I hug her back and pat her shoulder a couple of times to wordlessly tell her, "No, don't worry. I'm not here for that."

Ben walks through the foyer and into the sanctuary. He limps along, leaning on a cane, left arm up to his chest and left eye staring off to the side, though I'm pretty sure he notices me with his right eye.

I pretend not to see him and keep my eyes fixed to

the right of the main aisle as he shuffles toward the front of the church. Jackie wants to know what we're doing here, and I act like I'm too preoccupied with answering her to notice Ben.

I'm desperate to break the tension. I almost shout, "Wasn't I supposed to walk down this aisle toward *you*?" but I don't think anyone in the room would find the humor in it, except maybe Angela, but she definitely wouldn't approve.

When he's finally even with me, I dare to face him. "Hey," I say, even though I know it's inadequate.

"Hey," he says back.

He doesn't pause, but keeps moving past me until he settles into the first pew—my old pew—and sits with his back to us.

Jackie explains us to her friend. "Their father used to be the pastor here."

I nod. "We basically grew up here."

Ben sits mute in his pew, head tilted toward the floor, as Angela and I give irritatingly vague answers to the questions we're asked.

I'm torn between bragging about my amazing life and telling them how hard it's been for me. Both are true, and both frame a certain narrative I don't want them to hear. If I tell them about all the good experiences I've had, they'll think what they did—or failed to do—wasn't a big deal. If my life turned out so great, then what happened here couldn't have been so bad. I'm willing to forgive, but that's not the same as excusing what they did.

Of course, I don't want them to think my life's been one big ball of suck either. I can't tell them that, every once in a while, I have panic attacks. And I really don't want to touch on the three colleges I dropped out of. The prideful part of me wants them to think I'm so amazing and independent that I easily overcame what happened here. I don't need them, and I never did.

Angela's a little more forthcoming than I am. She tells them she recently finished her bachelor's degree. It's a big deal, she says, because she only got her GED. She explains that she had problems with her high school credits transferring when we left. I'm proud of her for the little poke of reality she's given them, especially since she's more sympathetic than I am around here.

Paul invites us to stay for Sunday school and the service. We hem and haw for a minute. I want to stay. I don't want to stay. I want *them* to want me to stay. In the end, we slide into the second pew from the back while Paul hands out the Sunday school booklets. The lesson is on Israel's neglect of those in need, which I think is funny, given the circumstances.

Each of us reads our assigned verse and speaks a little about what it means. Angela skips her turn, but I read Amos 6:8 (the King James version, of course) out loud.

The Lord God hath sworn by himself, saith the Lord the God of hosts, I abhor the excellency of Jacob, and hate his palaces: therefore will I deliver up the city with all that is therein.

"What do you get out of that?" Paul asks.

"There are always consequences for the things we

do," I say.

Jackie shifts in her seat, and Paul brightens. "You hit it on the head. There are always consequences for being disobedient."

I wonder if he's thinking about their disobedience or mine.

We finish the lesson right before Ben's wife and four children filter in to sit next to him. Paul steps up onto the small stage and formally welcomes everyone, especially the two guests. "You know, Angela, I remember the first thing you said when your family came to visit. You looked out in that field"—he points toward what used to be a fenced in area behind the parsonage—"and you asked, 'Who do those horses out there belong to?'"

He smiles down at her, and she chuckles. I remember it too, but I'm surprised Paul does. They were Scott and Jackie's horses, and Jackie told us if Dad came here to be the pastor, we could saddle them up and ride any time we wanted, which was what had sold Angela on the move.

He opens the floor to prayer requests. Jackie has a request. She and her youngest son have been fighting a cold, and she wants Paul to pray for them because "the prayers of a righteous man availeth much."

As Paul prays, I owl my head around the room, not even bothering to be sneaky about it. Everything looks the same. The same red pews. The same hymnals. The same podium. The same mailboxes. My heart skips, and I whip back to the front of the church. Phantom paper crinkles under my fingers as I read my name pasted over and over on an obituary.

We all stand and sing hymns that are foreign to me. They sound melancholy. With so few people, my voice carries more than I'm comfortable with. It feels wrong. I remember so much energy in that tiny sanctuary, but I don't feel it now.

Ben's children walk onto the stage and begin a song. As they sing, I count fifteen adults sitting in the pews. We were flirting with just under a hundred when we left.

While counting, I notice one thing *has* changed. The altar's gone. It always sat at the front of the church, but now it's missing. After a thorough search from my seat, I finally spot it shoved off to the side of the room. They've shown it no more respect than an end table. I try to remember churches like this don't believe there's anything particularly holy about the sanctuary or the altar. To them it's just a room and a piece of furniture. But it had always been God's altar to me, and it makes my chest hurt to see it pushed out of the way and forgotten, like it doesn't even matter. The day we left, I showered that altar in tears and prayed for a miracle. *Please God, save us.*

The children finish their song, and I clap louder than I probably should. Ben makes his way to the pulpit—my father's pulpit—and starts his sermon. It's Father's Day, so he preaches about fathers and how they always try to protect their children.

He and I know something about fathers. My father abandoned the pulpit Ben's preaching from because

Ben's father wouldn't ask Ray to leave. If we'd had some support from the assistant pastor, where would we all be now?

Elmer could have asked Ray to stop attending for a while. He could have suggested the church pay to install a security system in the parsonage. He could have offered to let me stay in the spare bedroom at his house until our home wasn't being broken into anymore. But he didn't do any of those things. He told Dad it was either preach to the man you believe is threatening your daughter or get out. So, we got out.

I glance back at the clock on the wall behind me, and it hits me that Angela and I are sitting in the second pew from the back, piano side. We're sitting in the same spots we occupied on our last Sunday here. I sat right here, in front of Ben and my friends, as Dad projected death threats onto the overhead screen while Ray smiled at me and Angela gripped my hand.

A panic attack's starting to rear up, and I do my best to swallow it down. This is one of the reasons I'm here. I've been known to pull a U-turn in a church parking lot on Sunday morning and head on home. Churches feel dangerous to me, and it's a feeling I'm trying to shake. I figure if I can make it through a service in this church, in this pew, with these people, I can make it through a church service anywhere.

I take some deep breaths and try to focus on the other reason I've come back. I'm not here to make smartass comments or demand apologies I know I'll never get. I'm here to pray.

An image pops into my head of a heavy millstone tethered to the underside of this sanctuary, dragging it down as it swings like a pendulum, marking off sins like time. What I've started to realize is I can't be the only one suffering from what happened here. There's no way these people got away without spiritual wounds of their own. When I mentioned it to Angela, she agreed.

Years ago, I fantasized about a millstone dragging them all down so they'd have to pay for what they did. I wanted them to hurt the way I'd been hurt, but I'm sick of people being hurt. Now, I want peace. But that can't happen without healing the spiritual wound on this place and on these people.

In the hotel room this morning, I scrolled through a prayer app on my iPod, searching for the perfect prayer that would eloquently say all the things I wanted to say, but I guess there isn't much demand for prayers that address predators and enabling church members.

As Ben continues to preach, I pray the only prayer there really is. I move my eyes to each person in the sanctuary and silently recite the Lord's Prayer. *Forgive us our sins, as we forgive those who sin against us.*

Ben finishes, and the service is dismissed. Angela and I stand up and are immediately surrounded, just like we'd been on our last Sunday. Jackie's face lights up as she asks if we've really come all the way here just to visit the church. I tell her we haven't, and it's true because we spent yesterday in Branson.

Ben hangs back for a minute before approaching us. It hits me how difficult it might be for him to preach to me, and I feel like a huge bitch. "You did a good job," I say as he walks up.

He bobs his head in acknowledgment. "Praise the Lord."

Angela chimes in. "You're doing something really good here."

"Praise the Lord," he repeats, like it's the only safe phrase he knows.

"I heard about your dad," I say. "I'm sorry." I may have had my issues with Elmer, but I didn't wish him dead, and I don't wish Ben the pain of losing his father.

He seems surprised for a second, then gives me a genuine smile. "Thanks. He's in a better place now."

I'm a little disappointed that he's reciting all the correct answers. I want to talk with my old friend Ben, not Pastor Ben, but his sister and mother are standing right beside us. He reaches his good hand out to shake mine, but it's more of a squeeze than a shake. "It's good to see you," he says, and he even sounds like he might mean it.

"It's good to see you too." And I mean it.

I've hugged every old church member in the sanctuary by this time, but I don't hug Ben. He holds my hand in his until I pull back, but he doesn't wrap his good arm around me, and I don't reach for him, even though he's my old friend and if it was anyone else, I would. But his mother and sister are crowded around us, and his wife is around here somewhere, and I'm not sure how she'd feel about her husband's ex hugging him.

I ask about his children and tell him they're cute.

Angela mentions my two girls, and I show Ben a picture of them on my iPod. He stares at it, gives a small smile and says, "Beautiful." He doesn't look away until I click off the iPod I was holding up for him.

We don't know what to say after that. There are too many dangerous topics. I say, "We're flying out of Little Rock this afternoon, so I think we're going to grab a bite and head down."

"It really is good to see you," Ben repeats.

"Same here."

Sixteen years ago, we stood right here and said our last good-bye, and that's starting to get to me. From his perspective, I up and disappeared for sixteen years until showing back up today after the church has all but died and he suffered a stroke. He probably hasn't even thought about me in the past decade. None of them have.

I can't keep standing around, waiting for words I know I'll never hear. Words none of them will, or maybe can, give me. Angela and I already had a brief conversation about realistic expectations. We know we won't get any apologies or any acknowledgement of wrongdoing. And that's OK because, although it'd be nice to get one, I don't need an apology. I can make my peace with these people without it.

"Bye," I say, and give Ben a smile.

I don't turn back as I walk ahead of Angela, into the foyer, and out the front doors. She stops me on the outside steps, where we'd posed with Daniel and Ben for our prom pictures. She digs into her purse, pulls out her phone, and points the camera at us. "Say cheese."

"A selfie? Really?" I say, but I'm already smiling.

We stand shoulder to shoulder, on the front steps of the church and smile for the picture. "See?" She shows me the picture. "We look good."

We really do.

ACKNOWLEDGEMENTS

I want to thank my family for their support and co-operation. I couldn't tell my story without telling parts of your stories too, and I know that caused some pain along the way. Thank you for being brave and for giving me permission.

Thank you to everyone who encouraged me to write this book. Your support helped drive me along, even when things got so rough I started smoking again and chain-eating Wint-O-Green Life Savers.

I want to thank everyone who read early drafts and gave me valuable feedback. This includes the members of my writing group, who put up with me the most. I especially want to thank Melissa Fain, Leslie Dunnett, Damian Baker, Matthew Spoon, Cheri White, and Michael Wright.

I also want to thank the users of the r/Christianity subreddit. I found you all when I was just starting to dip my toe back into this whole Christianity thing. You were the first people who heard parts of this story, and your encouragement reignited my determination to write this book.

And a special thank you to *all* the Christians I've run across who were not total assholes to me. You non-assholes are doing God's work. For real.

ABOUT THE AUTHOR

Kristy Burmeister is a former pastor's kid, former southerner, and current inhabitant of the northern woods. When she's not writing, she's either obsessively researching her family tree or "accidentally" showing up at your house, just as you're about to serve dinner.

STALKING FACTS

- 1 in 6 women and 1 in 19 men have experienced stalking which made them believe they or someone close to them would be harmed or killed.[1] Someone you know has been, or will be, stalked.
- Two-thirds of women are stalked by a current or former intimate partner. A quarter of women are stalked by someone they're acquainted with, even though they never had a romantic relationship with that person. Only 13% of victims are stalked by a stranger.[1]
- 76% of women who are murdered by their current or former partner were stalked first. 85% of women who survived an attempted murder by their partner were stalked first. Only 10% of female murder victims are murdered by strangers.[2]
- Stalking is illegal. All 50 states have anti-stalking laws, but they vary from state to state and are difficult to enforce. This endangers the lives of victims. A clear, federal anti-stalking law is needed to protect victims.

---

[1] Michele C. Black et al., "The National Intimate Partner and Sexual Violence Survey (NISVS): 2010 Summary Report (pdf, 124 pages)," Atlanta, GA: National Center for Injury Prevention and Control, Centers for Disease Control and Prevention, 2010. (https://www.cdc.gov/ViolencePrevention/pdf/NISVS_Report2010-a.pdf)

[2] Judith McFarlane et al., "Stalking and Intimate Partner Femicide," Homicide Studes 3, no. 4. 1999 (http://www.victimsofcrime.org/docs/src/mcfarlane-j-m-campbell-j-c-wilt-s-sachs-c-j-ulrich-y-xu-x-1999.pdf?sfvrsn=0)

RESOURCES

Stalking Resource Center
victimsofcrime.org/our-programs/stalking-resource-center

RAINN (Rape, Abuse & Incest National Network)
rain.org
Sexual Assault Hotline (800) 656-HOPE